Be a
Better Hitter
BASEBALL BASICS

Buz
Brundage

Sterling Publishing Co., Inc.
New York

This book is not licensed or endorsed by any league, player or players' association, Alex Rodriguez, or Ken Griffey, Jr.

Photo Credits:
Photos of Ken Griffey, Jr., and Alex Rodriguez by Ben Van Houten—except pages 82–83 by Tom DiPace.
All other photos by Craig DeCristo.

Designed by Judy Morgan

Library of Congress Cataloging-in-Publication Data

Brundage, Buz.
  Be a better hitter : baseball basics / Buz Brundage.
    p. cm.
  Includes index.
  ISBN 0-8069-2461-6
    1. Batting (Baseball) I. Title.

 GV869.B78   2000
 796.357'26—dc21
    BRU
                                          99-087961

10 9 8 7 6 5 4 3 2 1

First paperback edition published in 2001 by
Sterling Publishing Company, Inc.
387 Park Avenue South, New York, N.Y. 10016
© 2000 by Buz Brundage
Distributed in Canada by Sterling Publishing
c/o Canadian Manda Group, One Atlantic Avenue, Suite 105
Toronto, Ontario, Canada M6K 3E7
Distributed in Great Britain and Europe by Cassell PLC
Wellington House, 125 Strand, London WC2R 0BB, England
Distributed in Australia by Capricorn Link (Australia) Pty Ltd.
P.O. Box 6651, Baulkham Hills, Business Centre, NSW 2153, Australia

Printed in Hong Kong
All rights reserved
Sterling ISBN 0-8069-2461-6 Trade
             0-8069-2512-4 Paper

CONTENTS

FOREWORD

Teaching baseball has been a large part of my life over the past 30 years. I have been blessed with the opportunity to impact the lives of many young athletes in those years. Some of those young men went on to become professional baseball players, and others went on to fine careers in fields as diverse as you could imagine. But I truly feel that the values each of those young men learned during their experience in baseball helped them in whatever life experience they chose to pursue.

I am excited to write the foreword in this baseball book because I agree with many of the principles discussed in the mechanics of hitting a baseball. There are some slight differences in my philosophy, but I think that's what makes us coaches—we all have our own spin on certain things.

This book takes you from the very basics on to the more intricate details of hitting. There are plenty of books on the shelves of your local bookstore that can do the same. The thing I feel that separates this book from most others is the emphasis it places on the overall attitude. Everything is positive. The book is replete with positive phrases that if you take them to heart cannot only help you to become a better a hitter, but have

an impact on your life as well. Phrases such as "If you believe, you can achieve" and "Positive thoughts bring positive results" are great lessons learned not just on a baseball field but off the field as well.

There are some wonderful drills throughout the book to help you develop the proper muscle memory in your baseball swing as well as great advice for the mental part of the skill of hitting. Take the time to read through the book and find the advice that best suits your needs as a hitter, then concentrate on getting better in that particular area. This book isn't going anywhere, you can always close the covers and place it on your shelf and come back to it a little later. I know that proper practice is the only way to improve, and *Be a Better Hitter* is filled with proper practice drills and techniques. Be a better hitter and, if I'm lucky, maybe I'll see you on the field some day!

Rod Soesbe
Head Coach,
University of Nevada Las Vegas

Assistant Coach
U.S.A. Baseball Team

PREFACE

In the 18 years I have been coaching amateur baseball, I have learned there is one constant—good hitters always play! At every level, from peewee baseball to the major leagues, if you can hit, you will play.

I have also learned what makes a good hitter. In this book, I will teach you the three most important fundamentals common to every great hitter that has ever played the game: a good grip, the proper stance, and a good pre-swing. These three things can be mastered by nearly every person in the world. It doesn't take any tremendous athletic talent and yet it is the vital common link shared by every great hitter. You will also learn why these three basic skills are important and how they help to build a powerful, repeatable swing. The full swing, the proper point of contact, and other physical aspects of hitting all revolve around these first three important fundamentals, which you must develop *before* you go on to the more involved chapters in this book.

One of the most repeated quotes in baseball is the one uttered by Hall of Famer Yogi Berra, "Baseball is 90% mental, the other half is physical." What he meant is that the physical part of baseball is the easiest part to master. Swinging a bat is one of the easiest physical acts in baseball. Hitting a pitched ball, on the other hand, is one of the more difficult physical acts in all of sports.

Without getting too technical, I will explain some of the mental skills that will make you a better hitter. The later chapters focus on what mental approach to have, analyzing the situation from the on-deck circle, as well as the pitch count and other factors that affect your success at the plate. There are a lot of things that are important to know as a batter, including when to stop thinking and just hit. Like Yogi also once said, "You can't think and hit at the same time."

If you follow the instruction and drills in this text and pay attention to the tips and photos, your batting skill will improve greatly.

I hope this book becomes dog-eared and sits on your bedside table like a trusted friend. The more you read it, the more you will learn from it. If you want to be a great hitter, the information in this book can get you there.

ACKNOWLEDGMENT

This book would not have been possible without the assistance of many fine people—some who have extensive knowledge about the world of baseball and others who knew nothing until their involvement with this project.

First and foremost, I would like to thank Mr. Charles Nurnberg of Sterling Publishing for his faith and patience, and to his assistant, Margaret LaSalle, for her continued support and encouragement during the many twists and turns that developed during the completion of this book.

I would also like to thank the current and former major league players that took the time to review this book for its content: Wayne Kirby, Marty Barrett, Jim Shipley, and Dave Revering.

As important is the time taken by current head coach of the University of Nevada at Las Vegas Baseball Team and assistant coach for the U.S.A. Baseball Team, Coach Rod Soesbe, who reviewed the manuscript and was kind enough to write the foreword for the book. A special thanks for finding the time in his busy schedule to take part in this project.

A special thanks to the coaches of the Southern Nevada Bulldogs Baseball Club—Bo Hash, Ed Detwiler, and Dave Campbell—as well as the players themselves—Jon Jon Lemos, Bryce Thurston, Chad Robinson, Kylee Hash, Geoffrey Campbell, Eddie Detwiler, Brett Garlick, Rance Roundy, Kevin Kreier, and Bryon Brundage, my son.

Samantha Marder, Alexa Lemos, Derek Brundage, and Jesse Williams deserve a very special thanks for participating in the drills.

To Brenda Roser-Eyre for her patience in converting my scribbled notes into legible words on a computer file.

To Denise Kee and Gloria Cutcher for their invaluable assistance in fine-tuning the file.

To Gabriel Troncoso for his outstanding job of transforming my thoughts into graphic illustrations.

To Ben Van Houten, team photographer for the Seattle Mariners, for providing the wonderful photos of Ken Griffey, Jr., and Alex Rodriguez.

To Ken and Alex for being so skilled at their profession that their fundamentals can be passed on to the young athletes that read this book.

To my friend Craig DeCristo for taking time away from the busy fashion world in Los Angeles to capture the fantastic photographs throughout this book.

Most importantly, a heartfelt thanks to my father for instilling in me the discipline, desire, and dedication to succeed in anything I choose to tackle in life.

chapter 1
THE GRIP

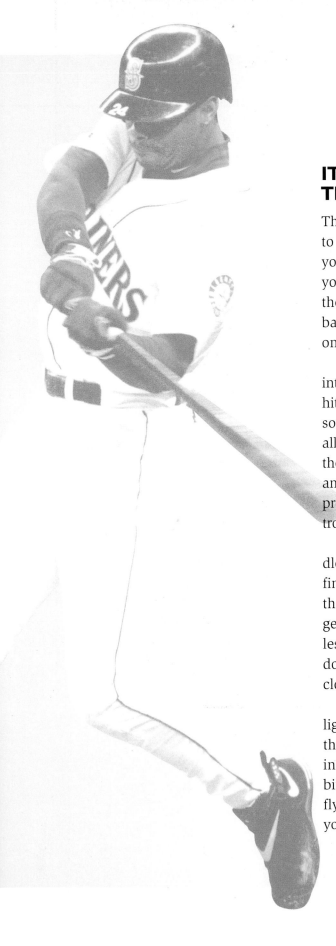

IT STARTS WITH THE HANDS

The hands are the only physical link to the bat. You don't hold it with your arms, your shoulders, your legs, your feet, or your mind. You may use these other body parts to swing the bat properly, but your hands are the only physical connection to the bat.

It stands to reason then, that if you intend to develop yourself into a good hitter, you start with a fundamentally sound grip on the bat—one that will allow your other body parts, once they are introduced, to work properly and efficiently with your hands to produce a powerful, effective, controlled, and repeatable swing.

A good grip is one where the handle of the bat is held primarily in the fingers of the hand. To do this, lay the handle of the bat across the fingers of each hand where the knuckles that you use to knock on the door are (Fig. 1-1). Then simply close your hands around the handle.

Do not squeeze the bat. Hold it lightly in your fingers. Pretend as though you are holding a small bird in your hands. You want to hold the bird firmly enough to prevent it from flying away, yet not so tightly that you harm the bird.

Fig. 1–1

A light grip keeps the muscles of the hands, wrists, and forearms loose and prepared for action. Loose muscles are fast muscles. You might think that by squeezing the sawdust out of the bat, gritting your teeth, and flexing your arm muscles, you are prepared to hit even a Nolan Ryan fast ball. In actuality, the reverse is true. Tight muscles are slow. The tightness keeps other muscles that you don't even realize you are using from helping you during the swing. Have you ever watched a major league hitter lightly grip and re-grip the bat as he waited for the pitch? He is unconsciously reminding himself to keep a loose grip.

The easiest way to ensure that you are keeping the bat up in the fingers is to rotate your hands so that the second row of knuckles on each hand line up with each other (Fig. 1-2).

NOTE

◆ ◆ ◆ ◆ ◆ ◆ ◆ ◆ ◆

Here is a great example of loose muscles being faster and more powerful: The next time you happen to be watching a boxing match on television listen to the announcers early in the fight. Inevitably they will comment on the boxers being "tight," that they aren't quite loose enough yet to "get off first." This is especially true during championship bouts because the fighters probably are a little more tense. Tension and tightness slows the muscles down. As the fight wears on and the fighters have adjusted to the moment, they begin firing punches with incredible speed and power. The tremendous quickness you see is the result of the muscles being more relaxed and ready to respond to the commands their brain is sending to them.

Fig. 1-2

The Grip

Fig. 1–3

make a believer out of you about the importance of holding the bat in the fingers.

If you are uncomfortable with aligning your knuckles as described earlier, try rotating the hands until the second and third knuckles line up with each other (Fig. 1-4). This is known as a "box grip" and is used by quite a few major league players. Either way, it is important to be comfortable. So pick the one that feels the best for your size and shape of hand, and stick with it.

Never hold the bat back in the palms of the hands (Fig. 1-3)! Holding the bat in this manner slows down the flexion of the wrists during the swing and robs you of natural quickness and power. Holding the bat in the palms can also be very painful. I have seen many batters, of all levels, strike the ball while holding the bat incorrectly and receive a terrible bruise near the web of the top hand. These bruises seem to linger with hitters for several days or even weeks. Believe me, it only takes one of these bruises to

Fig. 1–4

Both ways may feel a little uncomfortable at first, but it is important that you pick the one most suitable for you and practice it over and over. Soon it will become second nature to hold it in your fingers automatically. When that happens, you will have laid the foundation for all of the other parts of the swing to work effectively.

The grip is the first of the three, what I call, essential fundamentals you will need to master if you want to become a good hitter. Remember, the hands are the only body part connected to the bat. The bat is the only thing you have to contact the ball. Get this most basic of fundamentals down so that it is something you don't have to give any thought to whatsoever.

Some of the great hitters in major league history are said to have carried their bats around everywhere they went just to carry it, get used to feeling it in their hands, grip it, feel its weight, and feel comfortable with it. You can do the same.

The great thing about practicing the grip is that you don't have to be anywhere near a ballpark to do it. You don't need any extra space. All you need is a bat. You can practice your proper grip while watching your favorite program—or even better, while watching a baseball game on television. Study how major league hitters are holding their bats. Pay attention to how loose their grips are. You can learn a lot if you know what you are looking for.

Remember: Be loose, comfortable, and up in the fingers with the bat.

The Grip

chapter 2
THE STANCE

BUILDING A SOLID FOUNDATION

When it comes to developing a good stance, there are two very important factors that need to be expressed. The purpose of the stance is to afford you the best opportunity to see the ball and to provide you enough balance so that you can take a mighty swing at it. These two factors go hand in hand. That is, if you are in good balance then there will be less of a chance that you are moving your head around during your swing. If you are not moving your head, then you will see the ball better and naturally have greater success hitting the ball.

THE THREE STANCES AND VISION

As it relates to your stance, seeing the ball better means how you initially stand in the batter's box to look out at the pitcher. There are basically three different types of stance. The neutral stance is one where your feet are square to the plate (Fig. 2-1). This means that they are an equal distance from the plate. A stance like this affords you a good, comfortable look at the pitcher without straining yourself or otherwise becoming uncomfortable in the batter's box. Most major league hitters, such as Ken Griffey, Jr., use a neutral stance.

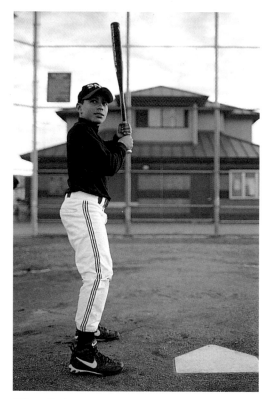

Fig. 2–1

The second stance, and also a very popular one with major league hitters, is the closed stance (Fig. 2-2). On the closed stance, the foot closest to the pitcher's mound is placed slightly closer to home plate than the other foot. The key word here is *slightly*. You can overdo most anything, and getting too closed with your stance will definitely hamper your hitting. The great Tony Gwynn believes this is probably the best stance for most hitters.

The open stance (Fig. 2-3) is just the opposite. The foot closest to the mound is pulled away from home plate. Jay Buhner of the Mariners is one of the more notable hitters that uses the open stance. Fewer major league hitters use this stance, because of the obvious distance it takes you from the hitting zone. An open stance requires you to do more during the time the pitch is on its way to the plate in order to get in the proper hitting position.

Choosing Your Stance

So which stance is right for you? Well, each one has its advantages. Before you choose one though, I'd like you to take a little test. Because it is important to see the ball well, we need to find out which of your eyes is the dominant eye. The dominant eye is the one that does the majority of the work when you look at something. It sends the messages to the brain about where the ball is as it relates to the space around you. Your other eye does the same thing, but your dominant eye sends more

Fig. 2–2

Fig. 2-3

Why is this important to you? The answer is simple: you want to make use of your dominant eye when you are hitting. Choosing the proper stance to help put that dominant eye to work is important. Ideally, your dominant eye would be the one closest to the pitcher: the left eye for the right-handed batter, the right eye for the left-handed batter. Unfortunately, most people are just the opposite. Right-handed batters generally are right-eye dominant and vice versa.

precise information. Remember, you want every advantage on your side—not the pitcher's.

Extend your hand out in front of you with your thumb up as though you are giving a friend the "thumbs-up" or "good job, way to go," sign (Fig. 2-4). With both eyes open, pick an object about 20 feet away from you and position your thumb so that the end of it covers that object. Now, close your left eye. Did your thumb seem like it moved over to the left? If it did, your left eye is your dominant eye. If nothing happened and your thumb is still covering the object, close your right eye. Did your thumb seem to have jumped over to the right? If so, your right eye is the dominant eye.

Fig. 2-4

Having your dominant eye closer to the pitcher contributes to better tracking of the ball to the hitting zone. This is one of the factors that helps explain why switch hitters hit better from one side or the other. Not having this luxury does not mean you can't be a good hitter.

The Stance

17

Fig. 2–5

What it means is, by knowing which eye sends the more precise messages to the brain, you should position yourself so that you see the ball with that eye.

This is the reason most major league hitters choose the neutral position as their stance of choice. I doubt, however, that many of them consciously know which eye is dominant. It probably came about from years of trial and error, and they finally settled on that position because they felt they saw the ball better. You can wipe out years of trial and error just by knowing which eye sees the ball better! From the neutral stance, you can position your head comfortably enough over your front shoulder to use both eyes to see the ball, bringing your dominant eye into play. Using both your eyes is known as binocular (Fig. 2-5).

Obviously, the open stance gives you an even greater use of both eyes. It is not used as often by great hitters because the trade-off for good vision and the increased amount of things you need to do to get in the proper hitting position are simply not worth it. The less complicated your swing is, the more successful you are apt to be.

The closed stance has advantages. If you can comfortably position your head over the front shoulder to use both eyes, you can take advantage of the increased plate coverage you get from this stance. Stan Musial, one of the great hitters of all time, used a slightly closed stance. If you were to look at him from the pitcher's mound during his stance, you might think his neck was made of rubber because his head was turned over his front shoulder. Needless to say, he saw the ball very well, and he hit the ball very well.

So pick a stance that affords you the best opportunity to see the ball well. Take into consideration which of your eyes sends the more accurate messages to the brain. You need to give that computer up there the proper information if you want to be successful at one of the more difficult physical acts in sports.

THE STANCE AND BALANCE

Now that you have decided which position you want your feet in, let's get you in a good hitting position with your stance. Your feet should be slightly more than shoulder-width apart, knees slightly bent, and your weight evenly distributed between both feet (Fig. 2-6). You should feel a little more weight toward the balls and to the inside of your feet. You should feel springy and ready for action, like a quarterback under cen-

Fig. 2–6

The Stance

Fig. 2–7a

Fig. 2–7b

ter. This is a well-balanced, athletic stance that will allow you to hit with power and grace.

The best way I have found to teach young hitters how to get into a good position is to have you stand with your feet about shoulder-width apart. Now jump as high as you can, straight up in the air (Fig. 2-7a). When you land, you will usually land in a very balanced and athletic position (Fig. 2-7b).

When you look down at your feet, your knees should be bent just enough to prevent you from seeing your ankles and the insteps of your feet. Standing too straight, or squatting too far, can lead to poor mechanics of the swing. There are obvious exceptions if you look at different major league players. Some crouch down, others stand straight up. That is a matter of "style" and that's something we don't want to discuss just yet. For now, balance and efficiency are what we want to concentrate on.

Mechanically, a good balanced stance allows you to freely stride with the front foot and rotate the back foot while maintaining enough balance to swing the bat through with leverage and power. Good balance is imperative throughout the swing.

THE HITTING POSITION

Now that the lower part of your body is squared away and you understand how to stand and the necessity for good balance, let's put the bat in your hands and get into the hitting position.

Fig. 2–8

Assume the basic stance position with your weight balanced and your knees slightly bent. Now, gripping the bat properly, raise your hands so that the top hand on the bat is just above and in front of your rear shoulder. The knob of the bat should be pointed down toward the plate (Fig. 2-8). The rear shoulder should be raised just slightly higher than the front shoulder. Your head should be turned toward the pitcher and looking out over the front shoulder so that both eyes are working for you. This is the proper hitting position. From here you are balanced and prepared to adjust to the path of the ball as it comes to the plate.

The Stance

21

Your Own Style

Every major league player has his own "style" when standing in a batter's box. Cal Ripken, Jr., has probably gone through ten different styles at the plate during his wonderful career. As I mentioned earlier, Jay Buhner has his own unique approach at the plate, as does Mickey Tettleton with his bat laid back nearly horizontal to the ground. Joe Morgan used to "flap" his rear arm like a bird just before the ball was thrown. Nomar Garciaparra, one of the great young hitters in the game today, shuffles and taps his feet back and forth as the pitcher goes into his windup. But every one of these players, and virtually every good hitter I have ever seen, returns to the proper hitting position at about the time the pitcher is releasing the baseball (Fig. 2-9). I call this the pitcher's "critical" position.

I have studied tons of film on hitters and I have found this to be a constant with every one of them. They might wave the bat around high in the air like John Kruk, or lay it on their shoulder like Cal, but when the pitcher reaches "critical," the good hitter sheds his style and puts his body in the best possible athletic position (Fig. 2-8) to hit the baseball.

I don't care what style you have in the batter's box. You can do cartwheels in it before the pitch. But, if you want to be a good hitter, you'd better get in the proper hitting position at about the time the pitcher gets to "critical." Otherwise, your

Fig. 2–9

chances for success are greatly diminished.

Learn what that proper position feels like. Embed it into your muscle memory. Make it second nature to adopt the proper hitting position automatically when you step into the batter's box. Practice getting into it over and over and over. You don't want to have to think about this, or your grip, or anything other than seeing the ball and hitting the ball when the time comes. So, ingrain these basics to the point of making them automatic. Once you have mastered the proper grip and the proper hitting position, you will be well on your way to becoming a better hitter. These two fundamentals are so important I cannot over emphasize them. They are the foundation that makes the rest of the swing so efficient.

THE MYTH ABOUT THE ELBOW

I have heard fathers and coaches yell to their sons and players in the batter's box to keep their back elbow up. I'm not sure where this tip first came from, but I can tell you it is wrong. Having the back elbow up in the air (Fig. 2-10) changes the hinging of the wrists during the swing. This, in turn, changes the path of the bat (see "The Swing Plane," page 47)

as well as the leverage which affects the speed of the bat. The proper advice, which may have gotten lost in translation years ago, is for the batter to make sure that his back shoulder is slightly higher than the front. The forearms should actually be in a reverse "V" and fairly close to the body (Fig. 2-11). This allows the bat to flow freely to the ball. This is explained in greater detail later in the book. In the meantime, practice the stance you see in Figs. 2-8 and 2-11, and you'll be well on your way to becoming a great hitter.

Fig. 2–10

Fig. 2–11

The Stance

23

chapter 3
THE PRE-SWING

LOADING THE SPRING

In every sport it is important to have rhythm and movement. In basketball, the player bounces the ball three or four times at the free throw lane before taking his shot. In tennis, the server bounces the ball a few times before the serve while the opponent is moving, bouncing, and shuffling around in preparation to return the ball. Even in golf, the player wiggles and waggles as he stands over the ball trying to create some timing. Now let's stop and think about this for a second. The golf ball isn't even moving! The basket isn't moving! Hmmm... Something tells me that if I want to be successful at hitting a baseball, which is traveling anywhere from 50–90 miles per hour, I might want to have my muscles loose and moving *before* the ball gets to me. This movement is the pre-swing.

To be a good hitter you must have loose, relaxed muscles (see page 10). The pre-swing helps prime your muscles for action because your brain is already sending messages to them. Then, when your brain sends the big command (SWING!), your muscles can react quicker and increase the probability of your hitting the ball. Learning a good pre-swing motion is as important to good hitting as the proper grip and stance. These three tie into one thoughtless process that helps transform you into a better hitter. Unconsciously, your mind is free to "see the ball... hit the ball," as Pete Rose once said.

The ideal pre-swing motion is a very small, semicircular motion of the hands coupled with a slight rhythmic shifting of the upper and lower body. The feet don't move, but you can feel the weight ever so slightly shifting from the inside of one foot to the inside of the other. Think of it as being similar to the golfer's waggle—only, instead of holding a golf club down, you are holding a bat up. All of this is done before and during the pitcher's windup as you are concentrating on seeing the ball.

The final motion in the pre-swing is when the pitcher gets in the "critical" portion of his delivery (Fig. 2-9). The hands come back away from the pitcher in a small movement (Fig. 3-1), the weight stays primarily on the inside of the rear foot, and you begin to lift the front foot (Fig. 3-2). This is the "load" position. You are ready to release your swing at the ball. Many batters actually build a small angled mound for their rear foot as they "dig in" the batter's box. This is something you would like to avoid. The angled foot tends to create a collapse in the mechanics of the swing. Instead, try this: Scrunch your big toe down into the ground. This will naturally place more weight to the inside of your foot and you won't have a tendency to collapse your back knee forward, which robs you of the ability to rotate properly.

Fig. 3–1

Fig. 3–2

Practice this pre-swing motion a few times on your own. You don't need to have a bat in your hand to do it. Pretend it is like a dance step. Get in your stance. Make sure you are balanced and the weight is distributed properly as we discussed in Chapter 2. Now, holding your hands as though you were holding a bat, make three or four slow, rhythmic motions and finish with a "loading" of the hands to the rear. Stop. Is your weight on the inside of the rear foot? Is your front foot still touching the ground, but barely, and poised to step forward? Do your hands feel "loaded" and ready to explode? Do you see how your front shoulder moves in toward the plate? You are coiled and ready to release a tremendous amount of energy from this position. Do this over and over without a bat until you become comfortable. Then add the bat. Get the proper grip and begin. Repeat this over and over again. I cannot stress enough that these three things are the basics to being a good hitter. You haven't even swung a bat yet, but you are becoming a better hitter.

All great hitters incorporate the pre-swing "loading" of the hands. Some are more obvious in their motion than others, but they all do it. Pete Rose, statistically one of the greatest hitters to ever play, had a very short "load" of his hands and a very compact swing. Paul Molitor has a similar motion—very short and quick. Because of their quickness, their "loading" was done at the last second, while the ball was nearly halfway to the plate (see "Timing," page 49).

Ted Williams, on the other hand, had a much larger motion. His hands would start up around his armpit and drop down and back as the pitcher delivered the ball. His hands would actually end up down near his waist before he finally raised them to the hitting position and exploded toward the ball with great bat speed and power.

Stan Musial, a great hitter and Hall of Famer, actually seemed to move his body forward first, timing his step toward the pitcher, as his hands just sort of floated in space behind him. They still ended up "loaded," but they seemed to get there in the opposite manner. He used the same principle, he just had a different approach or technique. The premier power hitters of the past, such as Babe Ruth, Hank Aaron, Roger Maris, Reggie Jackson, and Willie Mays, as well as today's home run hitters like Griffey, Mark McGwire, Sammy Sosa, and Barry Bonds, all employ the style taught here in this book. But they first did the three fundamentals covered so far in this book. They had a good grip, a good stance, and a solid pre-swing. Some were blessed and did them naturally, others had to work hard to develop them. But, they all did it. These three skills are absolutely critical to being a good hitter. It takes very little skill to ingrain these vital building blocks into your muscle memory. What it does take is desire to be a better hitter and practice. Be disciplined enough in your practice to use the proper techniques shown in this book.

Vince Lombardi once said that "great players don't do the right thing some of the time, they do the right thing *all* of the time. That's what makes them great." Practice doing the right thing all of the time.

The Pre-Swing

27

chapter 4
THE SWING

RELEASING THE SWING

The building blocks are now in place for you to develop a good solid baseball swing. There are some very important parts of the swing that need to be discussed. Understanding why you do a particular movement is as important as understanding how to perform the movement. First, I will describe a full swing. Then I will break down the important individual points in the swing and discuss them in detail. This will help you to understand why it is important to perform the certain aspects of the swing in the manner which I describe.

Let's examine a proper baseball swing (Fig. 4-1). As the ball begins to approach the hitter, he loads his weight to the inside of the rear foot and begins to close his front shoulder slightly. The rolling, or closing, of the front shoulder automatically cocks the hands back and puts them in the optimum position to release a powerful swing at the ball. Now the batter begins to shift the weight from the inside of the rear foot forward. The batter takes a *small* step *directly* toward the pitcher with the forward foot. As the front foot lands softly, the hands simultaneously reach their farthest point from the pitcher and begin their forward motion toward the ball. The rear shoulder remains

Fig. 4–1

up. The batter lifts the heel of the rear foot as the heel of the front foot lands and begins to pivot onto the ball of the rear foot. This is the same motion you would use to "squash a bug." The front foot is braced and "traps" the batter's weight, creating leverage to pull the bat through the hitting zone with tremendous speed. The batter finishes the swing and the top wrist naturally rolls over as the hands reach full extension away from the body, increasing the speed of the bat through impact. The follow-through brings the bat around the batter's body, with the hands coming up and over the front shoulder, which has rotated with the swing. The rear hip releases forward, leaving the hitter's belt buckle facing the pitcher. The batter should be in com-plete balance at the finish of the swing—front leg straightened and rear leg bent at an angle.

Study Figure 4-1. Then read the previous paragraph again while examining each section of the swing in detail. Visualize yourself making that swing in perfect rhythm and balance. These are the mechanics of the swing. It is extremely important that a hitter use the proper mechanics if he wants to have success. I firmly believe that if someone understands the reasons why he is asked to do a certain thing, he tends to do the thing better.

THE STEP

Up until the actual moving of the front foot, everything is pre-swing. The movement of the front foot is the mechanism that initiates the swing process. And, although we call it a step, in actuality it is not. The step is like a timing device, or a kick start for the swing. Something to get it started. When you take a step during walking, you transfer virtually all of your body weight onto the foot you are stepping with. This is not the type of step you take during batting.

A batter should lift the front foot and move it about 6 inches forward directly toward the pitcher (Figs. 4-2a,b). Under no circumstances should the "step" be more than 12 inches. Because balance is an important aspect of being a good hitter, taking too big a stride will ruin your swing. A good way to check the length of your stride is to lay your bat down at your feet with the handle end even with your back foot. Your stance and stride combined should never be longer than the length of the bat you use (Fig. 4-3). Some hitters merely pick their foot up and place it right back down in an effort to maintain their balance.

When setting the foot down, it is a good practice to visualize that you are stepping on thin ice or a basket of eggs. You want to land that foot softly without much weight attached to it. You don't want to break through the ice or crack the eggs. You don't want to lose all of your power. If you come forward too soon with your weight, you lose all of that energy you stored during the loading phase.

Fig. 4–2a

Fig. 4–2b

The Swing

Fig. 4–3

It goes right into the ground. Wasted. What you want to do is transfer that energy into bat speed. You want to "trap" that weight and use it as leverage to drive the bat through the hitting zone with great torque and speed. Landing softly with the front foot helps you achieve this.

Also, as you land the front foot, try to land on the inside of the ball of the foot up near the big toe (Fig. 4-4). Just as you want your weight on the inside of your rear foot, you also want your weight on the inside of your front foot. This helps you to

"trap" the weight and use it to power the bat through the hitting zone with the leverage you create.

Finally, when you land, it is important to step directly toward the pitcher. When the batter steps away from the plate, even inches away, two significant things happen. One, he opens his hips slightly and, two, he opens his front shoulder.

Let's first examine the hips. Remember how hard you worked to learn how to store that energy to the rear? By prematurely opening your hips, you just gave away half of that energy. You "unloaded" your spring. There is one exception to this rule of opening the hips too soon: pulling the inside pitch (see page 54).

The second result of stepping away from the plate is the opening of the shoulder. What happens? You lose coverage of the hitting zone with your bat. Stand with the bat extended out in front of you (Fig. 4-5a) so that it is parallel to the ground. Now take a small step away from the plate. (If you've ever heard the saying "bailing out" or "stepping into the bucket," this is it.) See how the distance the bat reaches across the plate reduces (Fig. 4-5b)? You've just lost the ability to hit the pitch on the outside of the plate.

Typically, a batter that is "bailing out" will hit the ball with the very tip of the bat because there is less of the bat in the hitting zone. A weak ground ball is usually the result. If you discover yourself hitting the ball off the end of the bat frequently, concentrate on stepping directly

Fig. 4–4

Fig. 4–5a

Fig. 4–5b

toward the pitcher and keeping the front shoulder "in" for as long as possible before exploding your hands to the ball. I'll bet you start hitting the ball much more solidly.

Interestingly, if a batter takes a step just a bit closer to the plate, the consequences are not so extreme. There is no unloading of power from the hips, and the plate coverage actually increases. This is known as "diving in" to the pitch. The only drawback with this approach is the difficulty in hitting the inside of the pitch. It is the least of the two evils and is much more acceptable.

Drill

To ingrain the proper step into your muscle memory try this simple drill: Practice loading your weight to the rear, then taking that light step direct-

ly forward. Nothing else. Load, step. Load, step. Keep the front shoulder closed and the body cocked. Load, step. It's almost like a dance step. Get a good rhythm going... 1. Load weight to rear, close shoulder. 2. Step lightly, inside of front foot, keep shoulder closed. 1. Load weight to rear, close shoulder. 2. Step lightly, inside of front foot, keep shoulder closed. 1, 2. 1, 2. 1, 2. 1, 2.

SQUASHING THE BUG

The rotating of the rear foot up onto the ball (squashing) activates the release of energy you've stored, in the form of weight, during the pre-swing. This is the same energy Mickey Mantle used to pound a 5-oz. leather ball 565 feet from home plate! Will you be able to crush a

The Swing

baseball over 500 feet in the air someday? Nobody knows. Maybe.

This is such a simple move. I think every kid, at one time or another, has squashed a bug on the ground. They stepped on it with the ball of their foot and then flattened that bug into the ground, lifting their heel for emphasis.

I like to take my hitters off to the side and just have them practice "squashing the bug" into the ground. Really grind it in there, working those hips and having fun. Then I put the players in a fundamentally sound stance, without a bat, and have them emulate a swing in slow motion, being sure that they incorporate that squashing action with their rear foot (Fig. 4-6). The result is generally positive.

In boxing, there is a saying, "Whip the hip!" It's a subtle reminder for the boxer to use the bigger muscles of the body to deliver a more powerful, knockout-type punch. The same holds true in baseball. Don't hit the ball like a featherweight when you can hit it like Mickey, or Ken Griffey, Jr., or Hank Aaron, or The Babe himself. Just whip that rear hip through as you "squash the bug" and your power will increase tremendously. Go out and squash a few imaginary bugs—get the hang of it again!

Drill

Here is a very good drill to help you get the feel for the "squashing" action. Take your bat and place it behind your back, resting it on your waist. Hold it in place by pinning it there with your arms or hands (Fig. 4-7a). Widen your stance a little as though you have already taken your stride toward the pitcher. Lift the heel of the rear foot off the ground. Now pull the bat with your right

Fig. 4–6

hand (for right-handers) toward the pitcher. Simultaneously, rise up on the ball of your back foot and rotate your back hip toward the pitcher, "squashing the bug" (Fig. 4-7b). Practice it until it is as natural an act as chewing gum. You just might be the next Mickey Mantle.

NOTE

◆ ◆ ◆ ◆ ◆ ◆ ◆ ◆

Tiger Woods is a perfect example of "whipping the hip." He unwinds his hips faster than any golfer in the game today. Tiger also hits the ball nearly as far as any golfer in the game—and he only weighs about 170 lbs! How does he generate such power? By applying the principle of "squashing the bug." His rear foot rotates up on the ball, which unwinds the hips, which releases the energy stored during the loading phase of his swing. Granted, there is a difference in the physical act of "loading" in golf, but the principle remains the same. The energy is stored to the rear so that it can be released during the swing, creating the speed necessary to propel a ball forward with great power.

Fig. 4–7a

Fig. 4–7b

The Swing

THE FIRM FRONT SIDE

Hitting against a firm front side creates leverage. This leverage is the force you use to pull the bat through the hitting zone. When you take your step and begin rotating the hips by "squashing the bug," you want that front side to create some resistance. It does this when you flex the front leg, resisting the weight from fully transferring from the rear foot (where we stored it) to the front foot. In essence, you "trap" the weight in the middle and rotate around it. Look at Figure 4-8.

Imagine that you have a long steel rod running right through the middle of your body. It penetrates through the top of your head and runs straight down through the middle of your body until it exits from between your legs and continues down into the ground. You can't move forward and you can't move backward. But, you can rotate! This is the action you are looking for. Firm up that front side, imagine that pole, and rotate around it. Whip the hip!

Be careful not to fall into the common flaw of pulling your front shoulder away too soon in an effort to pull

Fig. 4–8

Have you ever watched a football game and wondered how the kicker (usually a very small man) is able to kick the ball so far in the air? The next time you see a photo of a kicker in action, look at his front side. When he plants his front foot, he stiffens that front side and uses the leverage he created to drive the ball as much as 80 yards in the air! That is the same principle you use in swinging a baseball bat. Create leverage with the front side for better power and bat speed.

the bat through the hitting zone. I already discussed the consequences of the front shoulder moving away from the plate (see pages 32–33). Of course, it will rotate away naturally. Just be careful you don't "bail out" early in an effort to concentrate on creating leverage. A good way to keep this from happening is to adopt a mannerism similar to Matt Williams. Before each pitch, he touches his front shoulder with his chin to remind himself to keep that front shoulder in there and rotate—don't pull away!

If you doubt my philosophy about hitting against a firm front side, go dig out your baseball card collection. Flip through them and find pictures of your favorite major league hitters. Pay particular attention to the cards that show the player in mid-swing or at the moment of contact. I'd be willing to bet your favorite major league

player is hitting against a firm front side. He got to the majors because he hits the ball with authority, hard line drives, moon-shot home runs, and sizzling grounders through the infield. He hits the ball hard because he combines "squashing the bug" with a firm front side; he creates leverage. Leverage creates torque (the movement of a system of forces tending to cause rotation), which in turn creates bat speed and power. The result is a ball hit hard enough to get past the infielders, or to clear a fence 300 feet away.

If you want to be a good hitter, you must apply these two principles to your swing. You will hit the ball harder than your teammates that do not apply the proper technique. The final result will probably mean a spot in the starting line-up and the opportunity to help your team win some ball games.

The Swing

THE TOP HAND

The hands! The hands! The hands! Remember at the start of the book when I emphasized that the hands are your only physical link to the bat? Why then have I been feeding you so much information about the hips, feet, and shoulders? Because they all work together to make the hands work better. If you have naturally quick hands, they will seem to have superhuman speed through the hitting zone when you apply the principles we have taught up to this point.

If you have played under a good hitting instructor at any time in your baseball career, you have heard him say, "Take the hands to the ball!" Releasing your hands to the ball is vital to good hitting.

The top hand on the bat is the "power hand" in the baseball swing. It starts out on top (Fig. 4-9), trails the knob of the bat and lower hand (Fig. 4-10) as the hands "go to the ball," and eventually becomes the "lower" hand on the bat (Fig. 4-11) just before and during impact. The wrists "roll over" just after impact as the hands are fully extended away from the body (Fig. 4-12). The top hand then leads the hands into the follow- through, up and over the front shoulder.

Fig. 4–9

Fig. 4–10

Fig. 4–11

Fig. 4–12

The Swing

Drill

A good way to get the feel for this hand action is to pick up a small, light bat and hold it in your top hand only (Fig. 4-13). (I like to use the small collectible bats given away by many major league teams during promotions.) Hold it properly and in the proper hitting position. Place your other hand across your chest to get it out of the way.

Imagine a baseball sitting on a tee about waist high and slightly in front of your front leg. Take your bat directly down to that imaginary ball without rolling over your wrist (Fig. 4-14). You should be able to see your fingers, and the barrel of the bat should still be pointing some-what to your rear at an angle. This is a result of taking "the knob of the bat" to the ball. (This is almost the point of impact.) Keeping your fingers visible, flip your wrist slightly to bring the barrel of the bat down to the point of impact on the imaginary ball (Fig. 4-15).

To complete the top hand motion, roll the wrist over so that you are looking at the back of your hand (Fig. 4-16). Finish the follow-through by taking the bat up and over the shoulder. It is a good idea to incorporate the lower body action of "squashing the bug" when doing this drill to maximize your muscle memory of a good swing. Do not do this drill fast. Slow, smooth, and rhythmic movements are best. Be careful not to rotate your front shoulder away to bring the top hand into the hitting zone. The hand motion will

Fig. 4–13

Fig. 4–14

Fig. 4–15

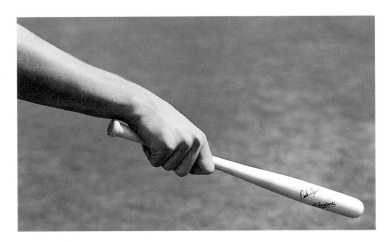

Fig. 4–16

naturally turn the shoulder during the follow-through.

Imagine striking a baseball at the optimum point of impact. Feel the point where your hand rolls over. Learn to time the "action" of the wrist and to make a smooth rolling motion. Repeat this drill at least twenty times.

THE BOTTOM HAND

As the top hand is referred to as the "power hand," the bottom hand is your "action hand." It leads the way and provides the action in your swing. In fact, the great George Brett (and other hitters taught by hitting guru Charley Lau) so strongly believed that the bottom hand was the important hand in the baseball swing that he would actually release the top hand at or near the point of impact and finish the swing with only the bottom hand. I do not advocate this and believe that the top hand provides the power. However, it takes both hands working together to create a much more effective swing.

Drill

Let's analyze the role of the bottom hand. Place the small bat in your bottom hand only. Place your off-hand across your chest to get it out of the way. Imagine the ball on the same

The Swing

41

tee. Take the knob of the bat directly to the ball. You should be looking straight down at the knuckle on your thumb (Fig. 4-17). Now make the same "action" motion with your wrist to take the barrel of the bat to the impact area. You should see the back of your hand and the knuckles should be pointing away from you

(Fig. 4-18). To complete the motion, simply roll the wrist and forearm (Fig. 4-19) and continue the follow-through up and over the shoulder.

Do this drill with slow, smooth, and rhythmic motions. Concentrate on the point of impact and the smooth transition in and through that vital area of the baseball swing.

Fig. 4–17

Fig. 4–18

Fig. 4–19

HANDS-TO-BALL DRILLS

To further ingrain the action of taking your hands to the ball, try these simple drills. They are designed to create muscle memory and instill the proper hand action in the baseball swing.

Soft Tap

Enlist the help of your father, brother, or a friend. You will need a Wiffle ball or other soft ball. Have your training partner toss the ball up softly in front of you. From a good, funda-

mentally sound batting stance, try to hit the ball with the knob of your bat. Take the knob of the bat directly at the ball and just tap it (Fig. 4-20). Be sure to incorporate your lower body action into the drill. Repeat until you are proficient and are using smooth, rhythmic motions to the ball.

If you have a small enough bat available, you can progress in this drill to a one-handed soft toss. Alternate your top-hand drill and bottom-hand drill while incorporating the action of striking a softly tossed

Fig. 4–20

Fig. 4–21

ball into the drill. This is an excellent training method and will develop tremendously active hands through the hitting zone as well as improve your hand–eye coordination. The result will be pure striking of the ball at the optimum point of impact—something every hitter strives for.

Fence Drill

The next logical drill to reinforce the proper hand action is swinging the bat with both hands. This drill will help you to get the right feel for the proper path of the bat to the hitting zone. Remember, all of the essential fundamentals discussed earlier must be adhered to: grip, stance, pre-swing, rhythm, etc., during these drills. Stand facing a fence as shown in Fig. 4-21, holding your back arm straight out so that the tips of your

Fig. 4–22

fingers just touch it. Now, with bat in hand and using the proper fundamentals, swing the bat through the hitting zone, concentrating on taking your hands "to the ball" (Fig. 4-22).

The Swing

The tip of the bat should not hit the fence. If it does, you will get immediate negative feedback. Hitting the fence is a result of "casting" or "sweeping" your hands through the hitting zone. Take the hands directly at the ball (an inside path), then be sure to "squash the bug," hit against a firm front side, and bring the wrist action into the swing. Finish high and over the front shoulder with your belly button facing the imaginary pitcher.

Remember, every time you swing the bat, swing it correctly. Muscle memory is powerful. Use it to your advantage. Make your muscles remember a perfect swing when you practice and come game time, when your muscles are "reacting," your swing will be functional, beautiful to watch, and fundamentally sound. Perfect practice makes perfect.

Chair Drill

There's one more drill to emphasize the importance of the hands to the ball. This drill can be included with a soft toss, if you choose, but it is very effective even without the luxury of hitting a ball during the drill. Find yourself an old plastic chair, or a bucket with a lid, and sit on it. Lock your ankles around the legs of the chair or base of the bucket. This is to anchor yourself into the chair. We want to eliminate the lower body action in this drill. The only part of your body moving will be from the waist up. Take your bat and get in the hitting position (Fig. 4-23). If you

Fig. 4-23

have the luxury of a practice partner, have him toss a ball up into the hitting zone. Take your hands directly at the ball, concentrating on the proper wrist action into and through the hitting zone. Finish high and over the shoulder.

THE FOLLOW-THROUGH

If you get into the habit of making a complete follow-through during every practice swing, you will increase your bat velocity during game situations. Your muscles will be trained to "release" all the way through the swing instead of putting on the brakes just after impact. It might make the difference between a ball hit to the wall and one that clears it by 10–20 feet.

Vin Scully, famous Dodger broadcaster, has a great saying about balls that make it to the wall but not over: "One more biscuit for breakfast and that baby is gone!" The suggestion, of course, is that the hitter just needed a teeny bit more strength and the ball would be a home run, not a fly ball out. I believe that the "one more biscuit" is in your follow-through. Try it, make it part of your swing.

If you are not following through after the swing into a natural release, which takes the bat up and around your body, then somewhere along the line you must be putting on the "brakes" to keep it from releasing. If you are putting on the "brakes," then you are hampering your ability to hit the ball hard somewhere. Look at Figure 4-24. Let's say I have a race car and I want to see how fast it can go. If I smash the accelerator to the floor and hold it there for one block, I'll be going pretty fast. But, if I smash the accelerator to the floor and hold it to the floor for two blocks, I would be going even faster! The same holds true for your baseball swing. Don't stop your swing. Accelerate it for two blocks, not one. You want your bat to travel as fast as it can for as long as possible. As a general rule, the faster the bat speed, the harder the hit! Accelerate! Follow through! Get that extra "biscuit" in your swing!

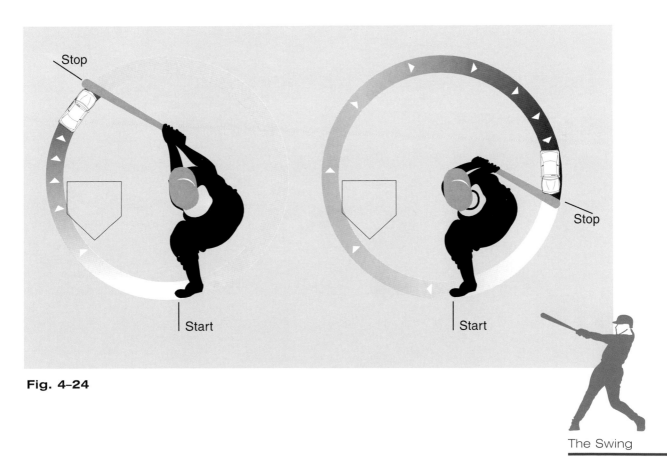

Fig. 4–24

chapter 5
MAKING CONTACT

THE SWING PLANE

Your swing must match the path of the baseball thrown by the pitcher as closely as possible, and for as long as possible, to successfully hit the ball. Pete Rose once said, "See the ball, hit the ball." Once you have ingrained the swing mechanics taught in the previous chapters, this is the proper approach. Let your swing take over. Swing the bat in the path of the ball, matching that path as closely as possible for as long as possible.

If all pitchers threw nothing but strikes for every pitch, and the strikes were all the exact same height and thrown from the exact same arm angle, and all had the exact same release point, combined with the exact same speed, with the exact same rotation on the ball (which affects ball flight), then and only then could a hitter have the exact same swing plane every time and successfully hit the ball. (This doesn't include the "timing" of the swing in relation to the speed and distance of the pitched ball.) It's no wonder that Ted Williams described hitting a baseball as "the single most difficult task in sports." Studies conducted by college physicists concluded that the batter is faced with tremendous odds for failure.

The key then is to have a good swing that is repeatable and

adjustable to the angle of the pitched ball. Since the pitcher is standing above you on a mound and throwing the ball from above his shoulder (most of the time), the ball will be traveling in a downward flight to the strike zone. Logically, the optimum swing plane for the bat would be a slight upswing to closely match the angle of the ball as it travels into the strike zone (Fig. 5-1).

Fig. 5–1

How many times have you watched a baseball game on television and seen the batter hit a low, inside pitch over the wall for a titanic blast? The replays show the hit and the commentator says, "Whoa, he went down and got that one," or "He golfed that baby out of here, it looked like a 3-iron going out!" These are perfect examples of the hitter matching the plane of the pitched ball with his bat. If the batter had "swung level" at those pitches, it would be a swing and a miss—Strike Three!

Your job as a hitter is to "see the ball, hit the ball." We have already grooved your swing so that it is mechanically proper. Trust it! Swing the bat in the direction the ball is coming.

The longer you are able to keep the bat on the same path as the baseball, the greater the chance you are going to hit the ball hard—probably over the fence, if you get it just right. If you get the bat "on plane" early in the swing, it has more of an opportunity to accelerate to the ball. The longer it is accelerating, the faster the bat gets moving (see Fig. 4-24, page 45). The faster the bat is moving, the harder you will hit the ball.

You only need to have the bat moving at approximately 75 mph to hit a ball 300 feet. Now 75 mph is really not that fast. Ever watch a golfer swing a club? Pros can reach speeds around 120 mph seemingly without effort. The swing we have built in the preceding chapters can easily reach 75 mph on an average 14–15-year-old boy. Most major league fences are less than 400 feet away in dead center field! These numbers, however, reflect a ball being pitched at major league speeds (more on that later).

Again, get the bat "on plane" early in the swing. Whatever that "plane" is. Many home runs have been hit on balls pitched out of the strike zone. Once you have committed yourself to swinging, give it a good rip. You have a good swing, so hit the ball hard somewhere. If you miss, so

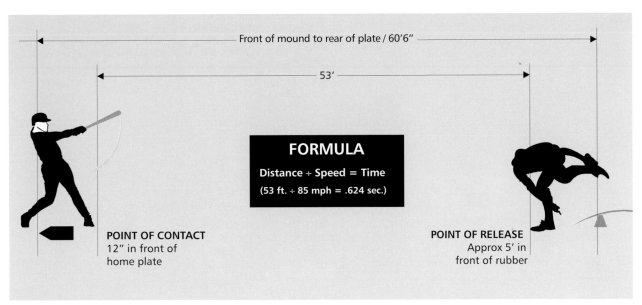

Front of mound to rear of plate / 60'6"

53'

FORMULA

Distance ÷ Speed = Time
(53 ft. ÷ 85 mph = .624 sec.)

POINT OF CONTACT
12" in front of
home plate

POINT OF RELEASE
Approx 5' in
front of rubber

Fig. 5–2

what? You get three strikes—more if you foul a few off.

I am not encouraging you to swing at any pitch. To be a successful hitter, you must be disciplined enough at the plate to swing at strikes, or what you believe are strikes. Not every pitch is a strike and not every hit is a result of a ball pitched in the strike zone. The batter that can best adjust his swing to the path of the ball is the "good hitter" I want you to become.

Ted Williams, one of the most analytical hitters of all time, really broke down the science of hitting with one phrase, "Get a good pitch to hit!" If you have developed a good swing with solid fundamentals, the moment you see a "good pitch" coming at you, let that swing go and hammer the ball somewhere!

TIMING

The next step in the act of successfully hitting a pitched baseball is timing. Time your swing so that it meets the ball at the proper impact point

and at just the right moment—not a moment too soon, not a moment too late. Hall of Famer Warren Spahn, while speaking of pitching, gave great insight into the art of hitting when he said, "Hitting is timing, pitching is upsetting timing." Hitting is timing! That seems too simple. How could it be so easily said? Because Mr. Spahn was referring to major league hitters and major league pitchers—people who should have the mechanics of their particular skills committed to muscle memory! Hopefully we have also accomplished this through the earlier chapters in this book. Or, at the least, you are well on your way to developing a proper swing into your muscle memory. At any rate, this is the time to begin understanding the art of hitting, not swinging. And the art of hitting begins with timing.

I have read numerous books on hitting and just about everyone gives a different time for the ball to leave the pitcher's hand and travel into the hit-

Making
Contact

ting zone. Some people say .4 seconds, some say .5 seconds, etc. The real length of time it takes for a ball to reach the hitter's zone is a matter of simple mathematics and can be easily understood by applying this basic formula: Distance ÷ Speed = Time (Fig. 5-2). So what does all of this have to do with hitting a baseball? Let's see.

If a pitcher is throwing a fastball at about 85 mph on a regulation size field, where the pitching mound is 60 ft. 6 in. from the *front* of the rubber to the *rear* of home plate, then it would take .711 seconds for the ball to reach the catcher's mitt, *if* the ball were released exactly 60 ft. 6 in. from the mitt. Since that is highly improbable, other factors need to be taken into consideration when determining how long it takes for a pitch to reach the hitting zone. Most pitchers actually release the ball from their hand approximately 5 ft. in front of the rubber. Using that number, let's subtract it from the 60 ft. 6 in. Now we have a distance of 55 ft. 6 in. The time it takes for the ball to travel that distance at 85 mph is .653 seconds. We lost about .06 seconds there, but that's not all. Consider that the optimum point of contact is about 12 in. in front of home plate and that the plate itself is 17 in. deep: 17 + 12 = 29 in. For simplicity's sake, let's make it 30 in., or 2½ ft. We are now down to a distance of 53 ft. At 85 mph, it takes a ball approximately .624 seconds to go from the pitcher's hand to the hitting zone. These are major-league–type numbers.

Let's look at little leaguer's times.

For 12-and-under teams, the pitcher's mound is 46 ft. from the front of the pitching rubber to the rear of home plate. Let's say a pitcher throws a 60-mph fastball: 46 ÷ 60 = .766 seconds. Hmmm, those are pretty similar numbers! Now factor in the distance we lose because of the release point of the pitcher, and the 2½ ft. from the back of home plate to the optimum hitting zone. Let's assume that little leaguers don't release the ball as far forward. Cut the major league pitcher's number in half by making it 2½ ft. That means we subtract 5 ft. from the 46 ft. and get 41 ft. Now, 41 ft. ÷ 60 mph = .683 seconds. Wow, that is only about .06 seconds different from the major league formula. That means that if you are a good hitter in little league, and you continue to improve your swinging and hit-

Fig. 5–3

ting skills as you grow older, there is no reason why you can't also be a good hitter in the major leagues.

As players progress through the different leagues, the distance between the pitcher and the batter gradually increases to 54 ft. and finally to 60 ft. 6 in. The formula remains the same however, and it is easy to see that the amount of time a hitter has to see the ball, recognize its path, calculate that information, pass it on to the muscles, react, and swing, is just a little more than a half of a second.

Here's more math: the average human reaction time is $3/4$ of a second. That's .750 seconds. What does that mean if a player simply reacts to the ball from the time it is released? That's right, if you are good at math, you figured it out. Go have a seat on the bench and Strike Three went right on by you before you could even swing (Fig. 5-3). Hitting is timing. A batter must begin his swing at the same time the pitcher begins his motion. There is an old saying, "When the pitcher shows you his pocket, you show him yours." In other words, when the pitcher kicks his front leg up to begin his delivery to the plate, the hitter should begin his "loading" or "pre-swing" motion, and prepare the bat for a swing at the ball. If he does not, it is physically impossible to react in time.

Learning how to time your swing is the art of hitting. If you work hard at developing a good swing by following the principles outlined in previous chapters, you have the makings of a good hitter. Understanding your swing and the rhythm and timing of it in relation to the pitch is the essence of hitting.

Fig. 5–4

When to Hit

Ideally you would like to contact the pitch approximately 10–12 inches in *front* of the front leg. This allows the bat to accelerate into the ball and the arms to be extended. When you extend your arms at the point of contact, you transfer a tremendous amount of power into the ball. This position (Fig. 5-4), sometimes referred to as the "Power-V," is the ideal position to be in at the point of contact. Again, I will refer you to your favorite major league hitter's baseball cards. Flip through them until you find him in the point of

Making Contact

51

contact with the baseball. I'd be willing to bet you see him in this "Power-V" position: arms extended, chin down, top hand not yet rolled over, eyes on the ball. Can you imagine the speed that bat is traveling through the hitting zone? Mark McGwire's bat speed has been clocked at 98 mph! Couple that with the impact of a ball thrown at 90 mph or more, and it's a wonder the ball is not physically out of round after suffering such a crushing blow!

Developing Timing

There is really only one way to develop the proper timing of your swing: batting practice, batting practice, and more batting practice! Hopefully you can practice against a live pitcher and not a machine. Machines are good, but not great. They can help you develop your swing and introduce you to a moving ball, but to really learn the timing of your swing, you need to see the motion of a pitcher and his arm, rhythm, and release point. Even Wiffle balls being thrown to you help you develop your sense of timing. Ask your father, brother, sister, or go out and play some wiffle ball with the neighborhood kids. Some how, some way, hit against a pitched ball. Develop timing. Hitting is timing.

TRACKING THE BALL

There is a direct relationship between seeing the ball and reaching that optimum "Power-V" position with the head down. It is called "tracking the ball" into the hitting

Fig. 5–5

zone. In order to reach that position (Fig. 5-5), the hitter has to see the ball leave the pitcher's hand, follow the ball with his eyes as it travels toward the hitting zone, and "track" it the final few feet by following it with his head. The actual movement of the head is so slight that it is almost unnoticeable. It is only a matter of an inch or so, but it is a very important inch or so. The difference in power generated from a swing with the chin down and "head on the ball" and the power from a swing where the hitter's head is looking off the ball is tremendous.

When you "pull your head" you may be lucky enough to hit the ball based on the initial swing plane of your bat in relation to the path of the ball, but it won't happen often. And when it does, the impact will likely not be very solid.

Think of it this way: when you pull your head, you stop looking at the ball. When you stop looking at the ball, your eyes stop providing information to your brain. Your brain is the fastest, most powerful, most competent computer in the world. But as great as that computer is, it won't work without receiving the proper information. When it stops receiving information, it has to guess where the bat and the ball "should" meet based on the last information it received from your eyes. If nothing changes—speed, direction, plane of the swing, etc.—from the last bit of information received, then you *might* still hit the pitch.

Doesn't it make much more sense to "track" the ball all the way into the hitting zone and provide your brain with complete and accurate information so that it can process that information and send the correct signals to your muscles, resulting in a greater probability of hitting the ball? After all, you haven't been working so hard on your swing just so you can swing at air. Nothing is more satisfying than seeing the results of your hard work pay off. Be disciplined enough to "track the ball" that last couple of feet. Don't guess. Give your brain all of the information available. You will hit the ball harder, farther, and more often.

One other very important factor in tracking the baseball is to try to keep your head level. By this, I mean when you are loading your weight to

the rear, be careful not to sit or "lower" yourself. Keep your back side tall and strong when you load your weight to the inside of your rear foot. Keeping your head on a level plane is vital in providing your brain with the accurate information.

If you "lower" your body when you load your weight back, you will look at the ball from a different angle than you were just fractions of a second earlier. Then, as you step forward to swing, you will most likely rise back up to the level you were before you began loading. Your eyes end up seeing the ball from too many angles. This usually results in a pop-up in the infield or a weak ground ball.

As you practice loading your weight to the rear, make sure you are keeping your head on the same level. Keeping your back shoulder up helps you accomplish this. Rock the shoulders back, but don't lower your weight onto your back heel. Dig in the ball of your back foot and concentrate on keeping a level head. Your tracking will improve, and you will get much more solid hits.

PULLING THE BALL

While we are on the subject of timing, this is the perfect opportunity to explain the concept of pulling the ball. It is hitting the ball to the left-field side for a right-hand hitter, and to the right-field side for a left-hand hitter. In order to accomplish this, the hitter must time his swing so that the bat arrives in the hitting zone a fraction sooner than normal. The ball should be from the middle

Making
Contact

53

Fig. 5–6

of the plate "in" toward the hitter. The reason for this is you actually want the bat head to not only beat the ball into the hitting zone, but to strike the ball almost on the farthest side of the ball (Fig. 5-6). The hitter must open his hips early on an inside pitch to accomplish this. This requires an early recognition by the hitter that the ball will be somewhere from the middle of the plate "in." It also requires an earlier decision to swing at the pitch, giving the bat sufficient time to beat the ball to the zone so that it can strike the ball from the proper angle. A ball that is "pulled" generally is hit very hard. Think of the race car example (see page 45). The bat has accelerated for a longer period of time, which means it has gained more speed.

More speed means more power. Even little guys can hit monster home runs when they pull the ball. Mickey Mantle slugged a titanic blast of 565 feet from home plate by pulling the ball!

As wonderful as it feels to smash the ball down the line, don't fall into the trap of trying to pull every pitch that comes to the plate. A good hitter hits the ball where it is pitched, including to the opposite field and straight up the middle where it came from. Take advantage of an inside pitch when you get one, but don't get "pull happy" or you may fall into poor hitting habits. Stepping into the bucket or early opening of the front shoulder are just two of the many faults that can creep into a good hitter's swing if he gets "pull happy."

There is not much difference done in the swing to pull the ball. The only critical thing the hitter needs to do is to start his swing early enough to hit the ball out in front of the plate. For the most part, the rest takes care of itself. The hitter does not need to learn a different approach to hitting or attempt a different swing. He merely needs to time his swing properly.

Pulling the Outside Pitch

Trying to pull an outside pitch is very difficult and there is such a small margin for success. It can and has been done throughout the history of baseball in many pressure-packed situations. For instance, in Game 1 of the 1988 World Series, Kirk Gibson hit the game-winning home run off Oakland A's reliever Dennis Eckersley. But it is should be left to very advanced hitters to attempt. There are just too many variables that must go right for the batter to be successful. The hitter must strike the ball well in front of the plate. The ball is in the "pull window" for such a short amount of time that it is nearly unheard of to hit for a high average. For the big, strong, power hitter like Mark McGwire, the risk is worth the reward. But for the hitter who consistently tries to pull the ball and lacks home-run power, this may not be the approach to take. Most often the result of attempting to pull an outside pitch is a weak grounder to the infield.

Don't take this to mean that you should not pull the ball. There are situations that arise that might dictate pulling the ball as the most effective way to help your team win. But, by and large, pulling the ball is the least successful approach to hitting. It is better to let the "pulled" ball happen during the normal course of competition.

Pulling the Middle-In Pitch

The ball pitched "middle in" (from the middle of the plate toward the batter) offers the perfect opportunity to get the bat head out in front of the plate and pull the ball down the line. Pitchers are not perfect, they make mistakes. If the game situation calls for you to pull the ball to help your team win, try to wait for the pitcher to make a mistake. If you are patient and disciplined enough to swing at only the pitch that affords you the greatest opportunity to pull the ball successfully, you will get it most of the time. Remember the great Ted Williams' approach to hitting: "Get a 'good pitch' to hit!" Well, that "good pitch" may differ from time to time, depending on what you need to do as a hitter during a particular at bat. As it relates to pulling the ball, a "good pitch" means something from the middle of the plate "in" toward the hitter and about knee high to waist high.

Drill

There are a few drills that help you develop your skill as a pull hitter. The simplest is the soft toss drill. In this drill, the person who does the tossing positions himself to the rear of the hitter and tosses the ball into the strike zone from the rear. The batter must not peek for the ball. He allows the ball to travel across the plate until it reaches the area most favorable to "pulling" the ball. The batter then "squashes the bug," rotates the hips quickly, and brings his hands to the ball. He does not follow the ball with his body. Instead, he tracks the ball intently with his eyes and explodes on the ball with quick hands and hips.

Being a good hitter is one-third having a solid swing, one-third timing, and one-third understanding the game of baseball. Now that we have covered the first two-thirds of being a good hitter, the swing and timing, let's move on to the final part of the equation.

Making Contact

chapter 6
UNDERSTANDING
THE SWING

HITTING FOR AVERAGE

"Going the other way" or hitting to the "opposite field" is an extremely important part of being a good hitter and playing the game of baseball. The ability to hit the other way requires the batter to make some adjustments in his swing. There are very few successful power hitters that hit the ball routinely to the opposite field. Dale Murphy of the Atlanta Braves a few years ago, Mike Piazza catching for the New York Mets, as well as Manny Ramirez of the Cleveland Indians are about the best I have ever seen. Surprisingly, although they hit the ball with power, they also hit for a fairly high average. Hitters that routinely use the opposite field are usually among the league leaders in batting average!

So pull hitters hit the ball very hard, but for a low average. Opposite-field hitters hit the ball for a high average, though not nearly as hard. Which type of hitter are you? Which approach should you take? Well, I'll tell you. Learn to hit the ball for average, to the opposite field, to center field, and occasionally to your pull field. Understand how to pull the ball, but don't live off of it. Later in your career, if you develop enough power to routinely help your team with a long shot, you can switch.

Tony Gwynn, as great a hitter as he is, didn't really start looking to pull the ball until late in his career when he was encouraged by Ted Williams to do so. Tony is now hitting some home runs when his team needs them, instead of a single to the opposite field or a double in the gap. Tony Gwynn has more batting titles than any man living (only Ty Cobb has more). He hits for such a high average year in and year out because he has a wonderful swing, one developed from the essential fundamentals, that he can repeat over and over. He has great timing, and he understands baseball enough to realize that his ability to hit singles to all areas of the field is just as vital to his team's success as Babe Ruth was to the Yankees or Hank Aaron to the Braves.

Rod Carew, Ty Cobb, Wade Boggs, Pete Rose, and many others understood the importance of hitting for average and made their mark in the big leagues. These men regularly collected 200 hits each season. That averages out to a little more than one hit each game! Sure, they had games when they didn't get a hit. Failure is part of the game. For the most part though, they put the ball in play nearly every time they came to the plate. They seldom struck out. They understood that swinging hard was not always the right approach. In fact, these hitters developed a style that allowed them to virtually hit the ball wherever the defense was the weakest. "Hit 'em where they ain't," is the way Willie Keeler described it.

Ty Cobb was so great at hitting the ball wherever he wanted that he used to routinely "spray" the opposing team's dugout with line drives during batting practice—more often if they were heckling him at the time.

Learning to hit the opposite way is what developed these legendary players into such great hitters. Learning to swing under control and practice, practice, practice, helped them reach their goals. You really can't go wrong with that approach.

OPPOSITE-FIELD HITTING

"Going the other way" requires a slightly different approach as a hitter. There is no doubt that being skilled in hitting to the opposite field has a direct, positive effect on your batting average. But the art of hitting the other way is a difficult one. That is why so few players are well known for this type of hitting ability. Of course, Ted Williams, the last man to hit over .400 for a season, was a pull hitter, so the theory that only opposite-field hitters can hit for high average is just that—theory. There are always exceptions.

The Four Basic Points

The basic concept of hitting to the opposite field requires the hitter to make four very important adjustments. The most important is that the hitter must allow the ball to either reach the plate before striking it, or strike it just slightly in front of the plate. Unlike the pull hitter, who could actually strike the ball nearly 2 feet in front of the plate, the opposite-field hitter must let the ball "get to the plate" before striking it.

There is a significant advantage in this approach that gives opposite-field hitters higher averages: the longer you let the ball travel to you, the longer you have to look at the pitch, analyze it, and determine whether or not it will be a strike. That extra 2 feet could make a huge difference in the action of the ball, and an even greater difference in where you decide that the ball and the bat should meet. The spin that a pitcher puts on a ball usually begins to affect the flight of the ball in the last few feet of travel. If, as a pull hitter, you need to meet the ball farther in front of the plate, you must start your swing when the ball is still quite a few feet from the plate. Hence, the spin has not yet taken affect. By the time your bat reaches the location you have calculated the ball to be at, based on what you last saw it doing in its flight, the ball has altered its course. Swoosh! Your bat hits nothing but air. Even if all of your mechanics are right, you may miss the pitch. This is why you get three strikes before you are out, and why the greatest hitters of all time failed nearly seven out of every ten times they came to the plate.

On the other hand, the batter that waits for the last split second to swing at the ball gets the luxury of watching the ball travel those extra few feet. He may see the spin on the ball and be able to better calculate where the ball is going to be. He

swings accordingly and strikes the ball into the opposite field for a nice clean single.

So the most important key to hitting to the opposite field is patience. Wait for the ball to reach you. Let it travel. Watch it all the way and then strike it.

The second key to opposite-field hitting is getting an outside pitch—from the middle of the plate to just off the outside edge. This is the ideal pitch to serve the other way, just as the "middle in" is the key to success for pulling the ball. By keeping your hands "inside" the ball you develop the proper bat angle to attack the ball and send it to the opposite field (Fig. 6-1).

Fig. 6–1

The third aspect of hitting to the opposite field is to swing under control, but with a *quick bat*! You must develop a quick swing, much like your approach with two strikes on you, to effectively hit the ball to the opposite

Understanding
the Swing

59

field. Cutting down on your hand movement during the loading phase is essential. Think of Paul Molitor's swing: very little hand motion backward and a quick explosion forward. That's the style of swing you want. Similar to throwing darts, you don't throw accurately by taking a big, long, looping arm motion. Your backward motion is very short and then you snap forward very quickly. You are intentionally allowing a speeding ball to get much closer to you than normal. You must be quick enough to overcome the time lost. If you aren't, then swoosh! Nothing but air.

You do not have to hit the pitch while it is in front of the plate if you intend to hit the other way. You can actually let the ball travel nearly halfway *across* the plate before you hit it. Notice I didn't say before you *swing* at it. I said before you hit it. If you wait to swing that late in the ball's flight, you will miss it.

The last part of hitting to the opposite field is hitting off a bent front knee (Fig. 6-2) and *not* "squashing the bug." I know that all along we have emphasized the importance of "squashing the bug." However, this is an advanced technique. In the Ty Cobb era, this was known as "slap-hitting." It should be no surprise that in his era the batting averages were much higher than today.

Hitting the Outside Pitch

The art of hitting an outside pitch the other way is to watch it travel, step to the first-base side of second

Fig. 6–2

base (for a right-handed hitter), lift the right heel, and push toward the direction of your step. Keep the left knee bent and swing down and through the ball (Fig. 6-2) with a quick bat. If you were to "squash the bug," the rotation of the hips would make it more difficult to keep your front shoulder in. Pulling your front shoulder away from the pitch is a sure killer for hitting the ball the other way.

By merely lifting the heel off the ground and pushing forward there is less rotational movement. It is more of a straight line. This "straight line" effect is more accurate. It is less powerful, but much more accurate. This is the style you will see hitters use when they are asked to execute the "hit and run" (see page 78).

Let me emphasize that this approach to hitting in no way negates all that we have taught throughout this book. I am merely explaining the "art" of hitting the ball to the opposite field. Some of you who read this section may decide that this is the approach you feel you will have the most success at. To others, it won't be your cup of tea. "To each his own" is a popular saying, and nowhere is it so appropriate as in hitting.

Drills

There are several drills to help develop your ability to hit the ball to the opposite field. Some of these drills require additional equipment, which may or may not be available to you. If you can't find the equipment shown in these drills, don't be discouraged. I have always been amazed at the ability of kids to improvise. Find a way to make do. But remember, never sacrifice safety!

Soft Toss

The soft-toss drill we used earlier to work on pulling the ball can also be used for hitting the opposite way. The "tosser" must be a safe distance to the rear of the hitter. The hitter must not peak. The "tosser" tosses the ball from the inside of the plate diagonally across to the outside. The hitter picks up the ball with his peripheral vision and "tracks" the ball with both his body and his eyes to the hitting zone. As soon as the hitter sees the ball come into his view, he follows it with his body by taking a stride toward the opposite field side of second base. He pushes off with his rear foot but does *not* "squash the bug" (Fig. 6-3). When the ball reaches the hitting zone, he swings with a quick bat and "strokes" the ball the other way. Throw your hands at the ball. On the follow through, the hitter should drop to his back knee to emphasize the importance of not squashing or rotating the back hip (Fig. 6-4).

Fig. 6–3

Fig. 6–4

Understanding the Swing

61

Inside-Outside Tee

The use of an "inside-outside" tee is invaluable in learning to hit the ball the opposite way and/or pulling the ball. To properly set up this drill, place the ball on the "inside" (approximately 8–10 inches in front of the plate) and the ball on the "outside" (right on the outside edge of the front corner). The "inside" ball should be about 4–5 inches higher than the outside ball.

The hitter gets in a fundamentally sound batting stance and begins his "pre-swing," loading his hands and body in preparation to hit the ball wherever it is "pitched." His training partner then announces "inside" or "outside." The batter attacks the appropriate ball using all of the afore-mentioned techniques (Fig. 6-5).

For the "inside" ball, hit off a firm front side and get good rotation of the rear foot with a balanced follow-through (Fig. 6-6). For the "outside" pitch, concentrate on stepping to the opposite field side of second base and lift the heel (but not rotating the back side). Take a smooth, quick swing at the ball with the hands on the inside of the ball and drop to the rear knee to emphasize the non-rotation of the hip (Fig. 6-4).

Fig. 6–5

Fig. 6–6

Fig. 6–7

Short-Screen "Now"

Another wonderful drill that can be used for both pulling the ball or hitting to the opposite field is the short-screen "now" drill. In this drill you must have access to a pitcher's L-screen. The L-screen allows the pitcher to move closer to the hitter without danger of being struck by a batted ball. It also improves accuracy, which maximizes the amount of balls thrown in the strike zone.

For the "now" drill, move the L-screen up to about 40 feet from home plate. To work on pulling the ball, the pitcher would throw two pitches toward the "middle in" of the strike zone (Fig. 6-7). Each time the hitter does *not* swing. Instead, he completes an overexaggerated hip turn, "squashes the bug," and begins the swing but stops. He yells out "now" at the point he believes the ball has reached his "pull window." On the third pitch, he executes the swing and pulls the ball.

For the opposite field, the pitcher throws two successive pitches to the "middle-out" portion of the strike zone. The hitter steps to the opposite field side of second base, lifts the heel of the rear foot, and pushes toward the opposite field. The hitter keeps his shoulder "in" and tracks the ball's flight just a fraction longer. He yells "now" when he believes the ball is in the proper position to stroke the other way. On the third

Understanding the Swing

pitch, the hitter swings away with all of the proper mechanics and finishes down on the rear knee. Again, over-exaggerate the shoulder staying "in" or "closed."

It is important to emphasize the proper fundamentals during drills. Overexaggerating a movement in a drill helps to build muscle memory for that function when it is needed in real situations.

It also helps if the hitter can picture himself striking the ball to the opposite field during the balls he calls "now" on. He will see a great deal of success on the third pitch when he actually does swing the bat. Never underestimate the power of the mind. It has been proven in many scientific experiments that visualization is powerfully effective in enhancing athletic performance.

Finish the drill by allowing the hitter to "hit away" at successive pitches. Concentrate on hitting the ball to the side you just completed the drill on.

INSIDE OUT

Learning to hit the inside pitch the other way is the most advanced form of hitting. Consistently striking the inside ball hard and directing it away is the crowning achievement of any hitter.

First, the hitter must understand what it takes to hit the inside pitch "out." You may be surprised to hear me say this, but the hitter does nothing different aside from having the discipline to let the inside pitch travel to him! The only physical difference in the swing is

that the hands are much closer to the body in order to remain inside the ball. The rest takes care of itself because of the angles created by the closeness of the ball to the hitter. Bat quickness is the secret! If you have a long, looping swing, you can't do this. You must take your hands to the ball quickly. Otherwise you will fail.

The most important aspect is for the hitter to lead with the hands. The bat barrel will naturally lag behind the hands. The hands *must* remain close to the body and *inside* the ball (Fig. 6-8). The bat barrel actually drags behind the hands and enters the hitting zone at a very steep angle. The hitter executes a normal swing. The difference in angles created by the closeness of the hands to the body results in the bat striking

Fig. 6–8

the ball on the "inside." The ball naturally goes the other way.

If a hitter tries to "chop" at the ball, as I have heard other instructors try to emphasize, there is too much thinking. You don't have time to think. Let the ball travel, get your hands inside the ball (Fig. 6-9a), and have a quick set of hands. Presto! An inside-out swing (Fig. 6-9b).

This technique should be practiced repeatedly with soft-toss Wiffle balls. The balls should be tossed waist high and in tight to the hitter.

Some of the greatest hitters of all time swear that when they learned this technique of hitting, it made them complete hitters and elevated them to greatness. One reason it can add to a hitter's average is that, at high levels of baseball, the defense is generally set in accordance to where the pitcher intends to pitch to the hitter. Most hitters "pull" inside pitches and, therefore, the defense is prepared for the pull hit. When the hitter is able to "inside-out" a pitch, he takes advantage of the defense's weakness. This could result in as many as twenty to thirty additional hits during the course of a season. Those twenty to thirty hits could make a significant impact on a batting average.

This is a learned skill, though—not one you are born with. You must practice this tirelessly because the inclination is to try to beat the ball to the spot and pull it. You must accept the pitch and let it work for you in order to "go the other way." Get good at this and you will be looked upon as a very good hitter.

Fig. 6–9a

Fig. 6–9b

Understanding
the Swing

DEVELOPING QUICKNESS

One important ingredient you must develop to be successful in hitting the ball to the opposite field is bat quickness. If you are going to watch the ball for a longer period of time, then you must have the bat quickness to beat the ball to the hitting zone. Bat quickness can be developed through a little discipline, desire, and dedication—the 3 D's of life!

You must commit yourself to doing the following training routine for at least 6 weeks. Less than that and you will not see much improvement. But you will see dramatic results for every week beyond that 6 weeks. Your body needs sufficient time to be "trained." Just as when you were first learning how to read, your eyes had to learn to recognize letters and your ears had to learn to remember their sound. It took a while. It didn't happen overnight. To be quick, you must "teach" your muscles what it feels like to be fast. It will take time, but they will learn.

THE WRIST ROLL

To develop a quick bat, you must have strong hands, wrists, and forearms. Some hitters are blessed with these qualities naturally. Others will need to work on getting stronger in this area. If you have naturally strong hands, wrists, and forearms, you should still improve on what you already have. You could be that much farther ahead of your opponent.

Have your father head to the hardware store and buy a column of wood about 18 inches long and approximately 3–4 inches in circumference. You also need about a 4-foot piece of nylon rope (Fig. 6-10). Drill a hole in the center of the wood and

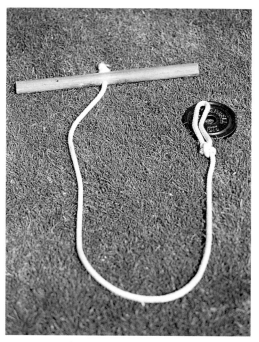

Fig. 6–10

insert the rope. Tie a knot in the end of the rope to keep it from slipping back through. On the other end of the rope, tie a loop. Go to your local sports equipment store and purchase a 2½-lb. dumbbell plate and a 5-lb. dumbbell plate. Slip the looped end of the rope through the center of the smaller plate and then slip the wood handle through the loop in the rope (Fig. 6-11). You now have the perfect device to build strong hands, wrists, and forearms. The entire device shouldn't cost more than $10 to make. But it is invaluable to your development as a hitter.

Fig. 6–11

Drill

On Monday, Wednesday, and Friday of each week for at least 6 weeks spend at least 15 minutes a day rolling the rope around the handle. Roll the weight up, then roll it back down (Fig. 6-12). Take a break after each ten times you complete the sequence. If you find that the 2½-lb. weight is too heavy, ask your father to buy you a 1-lb. weight and switch weights. Work yourself up until you can switch back to the 2½-lb. weight. Your goal is to be able to eventually perform this exercise with a 5-lb. weight attached. If you are very young, it may take quite a while before you are capable of doing this. But if you have the discipline, desire, and dedication to keep at this until you can attach that 5-lb. weight and complete the routine, your hands, wrists, and forearms will become very strong.

Fig. 6–12

For about the first 2 weeks, you will experience some muscle soreness in the forearms. That is natural. Your muscles are adapting to the workload. Stick with it and that soreness will be replaced by strength.

GRADUATING BAT WEIGHTS

This exercise is the key to creating quickness. If you have been playing baseball for a few years, you probably have a few different sizes of bats lying around in the garage. Go get them. They are your tools for success. Ideally, you need at least three

Understanding the Swing

67

graduating sizes of bats. A tee-ball bat (maybe 16 oz.), a little league bat (approximately 20–23 oz.), and a senior league bat (about 27 oz.). You also need a weighted bat or a device to weight your heaviest bat, such as a "donut" or "power fins."

Additionally, you need an extremely light bat, such as the mini collector bats. If you can't get one of these, you can use a cut-down piece of broomstick. You have to have this progression of weights in order to make this system work.

Drill

Set your "tools" in progressive order near you from lightest to heaviest (Fig. 6-13). Begin with the middle bat and take some smooth, easy cuts. Just loosen up. Take about fifteen to twenty cuts like this and get your muscles prepared to work. Do a little stretching to make sure your muscles are prepared before you stress them.

Now you are set to begin your workout. Again, with the middle bat, get in a fundamentally sound stance and imagine a ball in your power zone. Take a solid, balanced, but powerful cut at that imaginary ball. Concentrate on your rhythm, your loading, your timing kick, and your hands exploding to the ball. Exaggerate "squashing the bug" and the follow-through. Concentrate on finishing balanced. The perfect swing, that's what you want every time. Repeat this ten times. Set the bat down and graduate to the next heaviest bat. Repeat the same

Fig. 6–13

process. Set that bat down and progress to your weighted bat. Repeat. Concentrate on doing everything perfectly. Now, start back down the line of bats. When you get to that super-light bat, you should be swinging with tremendous speed. Bat quickness! Rip those hands through the strike zone with all of your might! Again, do not abandon form. Drill the proper form into your swing by concentrating on doing everything correctly. Finish balanced every time.

For the first week this is all you do: one time through the bat progression. The second week, go for two times through. From the third week on, try to get three "sets" in during each session. Do this routine Tuesday, Thursday, and Saturday of each week.

QUICKNESS PROGRAM

Wrist roll on Monday, Wednesday, and Friday. Graduated bat workout on Tuesday, Thursday, and Saturday. Rest on Sunday. You will be amazed at the difference in your bat speed and power by the time that 6-week period is over. I am certain that you will not be the only one to notice. In fact, I am certain you will be approached by at least one of your teammates and probably one of your coaches. They too will be impressed. That should be all the incentive you need to continue what you are doing. Dedication.

This drill can put a tremendous amount of power in your hitting *if* you are disciplined enough to do the drill properly, have the desire to turn yourself into a better hitter, and are dedicated enough to continue it even in the off-season. Make yourself into the great hitter that you want to be. If you believe, you can achieve!

Understanding
the Swing

chapter 7
BASEBALL IS
90% MENTAL

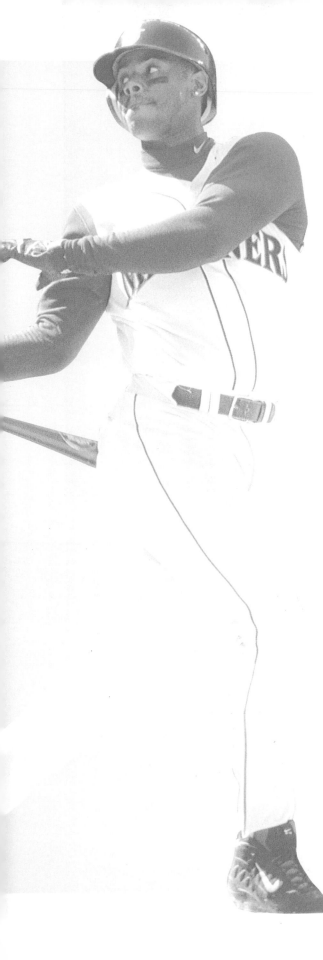

THE ON-DECK CIRCLE

As I mentioned earlier, much of hitting is understanding the game. Baseball is a game of situations. Because baseball is a team game, a successful at-bat may not be one that results in a base hit.

Your time in the on-deck circle should be used to analyze the game situation. How can you help your team when it's your turn to step into the batter's box? Will a bunt help the team? A fly ball? Should you try to hit the ball to the opposite field? These questions should be asked and answered before you step in to hit.

How many times have you watched a ball game on television and seen a player get high-fives from every player and coach in the dugout for making an out? It happens. Do you think they were happy about the player being out? You bet they were! If he got high-fives, he made what is known as a "good out," one that helps the team win.

Analyzing the situation helps you go up to the plate with a purpose. In and of itself, this mindset makes you a better hitter. Earlier in the book I mentioned the quote, "You can't think and hit at the same time." But you can think *before* you step in the box and you can think

before each pitch. The smart hitter is sought after at every level of baseball. Be a smart hitter.

How many times have you seen a ball player kneeling on one knee seemingly doing nothing? He may even be resting his chin on the knob of the bat. What is he doing? Studying. Perhaps the most important thing you can do as a hitter is study the pitcher. He is the one that controls the ball, the one that tries to fool you bad enough to have you strike out or have you ground the ball weakly to one of the fielders behind him. How fast is he pitching? Is his fastball in your comfort zone, or will you have to make some adjustments in your timing to catch

up to it? What else is he throwing? Does he have an off-speed pitch? Does he throw it differently? How about a breaking pitch? Can he locate it, or does he just throw it up there? What pitch does he likely throw when he is ahead in the count? Behind in the count?

These are all factors that you should pay attention to. There are a dozen or more questions you can answer in the on-deck circle that will better prepare you for each at bat. Remember the quote, "Hitting is timing." Having a good idea of what a pitcher throws in a given situation will make it easier for you to time the pitch and hit it hard somewhere.

One last thing about the on-deck

circle: Use that time to be prepared for your at-bat. Limber up and pay attention to the game. This is not the time to flirt with your girlfriend in the stands, pose for a picture for your grandma, or do anything else that detracts you from the game. Hitting is a huge part of baseball. Pay attention in the on-deck circle. You will be a better hitter as a result.

THE PITCH COUNT

The pitch count should have a direct impact on each swing you take at the plate. Certain pitch counts favor the hitter and certain ones favor the pitcher. Just as the smart pitcher takes advantage of the times he is "ahead in the count," the smart hitter understands when he has the advantage. In these situations, the hitter must capitalize. Or, at least, give it his best.

If you are ahead in the count 1–0, 2–0, 2–1, or 3–1, you should be looking for that "good pitch to hit"—something in your favorite area of the plate that you usually hit hard. Knowing your strong spot is crucial in this situation. If you have no idea where in the strike zone you hit best, then you cannot take advantage of the "hitter's count" situations. These are the times when you can really look for a pitch and when you get it, really take a strong cut at it.

Fastball Count

These "hitter's counts" are not only ideal situations to look for a ball in a certain area, but they are what are known as "fastball counts." The pitcher does not want to risk throwing

another ball and falling further behind in the count. So you will usually get a fastball in these counts. If you know you are likely to get a fastball, your likelihood for success skyrockets ("hitting is timing"). In addition, on 2–0, 2–1, 3–1, and 3–0 counts, that fastball is going to be "fatter" (thrown more to the center of the strike zone) because that pitcher does not want to give you a base on balls. These are pitches you should be able to hit to all parts of the ballpark with authority.

On the 1–0 count, although you are ahead, it is early and the pitcher may take a chance with a different pitch. Or he may throw a fastball to a certain location. Certainly, your level of competition and age group play a factor in what might be thrown in these situations.

Up to the age of 15–16 the tendencies that I have described are pretty steadfast. Above that, and on up to the major leagues, pitchers have much greater control of a variety of pitches and may be willing to risk throwing something other than a fastball on a "fastball count."

The pitch generally thrown at these higher levels is that particular pitcher's "best" pitch (which is another good reason to study your opposing pitcher while you are in the on-deck circle). However, studies show that a fastball is still the most likely pitch. Knowing that, and remembering that a large part of hitting is timing, you should look for the fastball. If you get anything else, unless it is so nice you can't resist hitting it, let it go by.

Baseball is 90% Mental

This is called being patient and waiting for a good pitch to hit. At the very worst, the umpire will call it a strike and you deal with the next count.

1-1 Count

If you are even in the count 1-1, or down 0-1, you must adopt a different mindset to be a successful hitter. Approach these counts with the idea that you are going to hit the ball "the other way." One reason for this approach is that you will naturally track the ball a fraction of a second longer, giving you more time to decide if the pitch is going to be a strike.

Additionally, this approach gives you the ability to hit pitches away from you, or on the "outside corner" of the plate. Pitchers like to nibble with borderline pitches to see if batters will chase them. If they do, the pitcher is in control. If not, he has to adjust. Pitchers generally like to nibble on the outside of the plate, as that is the most difficult pitch to learn to hit. At higher levels of play the pitcher will "come inside" to set up something "outside" on the next pitch.

A good hitter will look for a pitch in the "middle" of the plate and adjust "in" or "out." If you look "in" and get "out," you have to adjust for the full 17 inches of plate coverage. Whereas if you look "middle" and get an "inside" or "outside" pitch, the most you have to adjust is half the plate.

Two-Strike Hitting

When you have two strikes on you it is imperative that you take a "bat-

tling" mindset with you to the plate. This is "war" between you and the pitcher. Cut down on your swing, keep your head still, and intensely track the ball the moment it leaves the pitcher's hand. You want to hit it to the big part of the ballpark, right up the middle. Your goal is to "get a piece of it" if it is anywhere close to the strike zone. If you hit it fair, fine. If it's a real tough pitch in a tough location, foul it off. The more pitches you make the pitcher throw in these situations, the greater your advantage. First, the pitcher cannot remain perfect. Sooner or later he is going to make a mistake and throw you a good ball to hit. Second, the more pitches you make him throw, the more fatigued he becomes, which may lead to more mistakes.

Brett Butler was perhaps the greatest hitter I ever saw at "battling" a pitcher with two strikes on him. He could foul off more pitches that were just too close to let go by than anyone in the game. My philosophy has always been "don't let the umpire decide." Keep battling. Many hitters have been called out on a third strike that was "close." Don't risk it. Keep battling. Chances are you will get a better pitch to hit. This is "two-strike" hitting or "protecting the plate"—a totally different approach than when you are ahead in the count.

A good hitter understands the game well enough to adjust his mental approach on each pitch as the count changes. Nobody is encouraging you to be a "guess hitter"—just understand the game and its tendencies.

0–0 Count

There are two schools of thought about the first pitch. Some of the great hitters adopt the position that they want to look at the first pitch. See what the pitcher's got. Get a gauge for his speed, etc. Their thought process is that if hitting is timing, they will be in a better position to time their swing.

I believe in the opposite for two reasons: One, you should have been paying attention during your time in the on-deck circle or, if you are the first batter of the game, during the pitcher's warm-up. Study the pitcher and know him. He is your adversary.

The second and most important reason is this: Pitchers are instructed to get ahead in the count! "First pitch, first strike, first out" is drilled into them from an early age. It stands to reason that most first pitches are going to be "good pitches to hit."

I believe in treating the 0–0 pitch like a 2–0 pitch. Look for a fastball in your "zone." If you get it, smash it. Swing hard at this pitch. If you miss it, it's 0–1 and you have two strikes left. If the pitch is not to your liking, let it go by. The worst it can be is 0–1. Plus, you had a chance to "look" at one to see what the pitcher has.

Very often the first pitch in an at-bat is the best pitch you will see. If you live by the philosophy to always "take" that pitch, guess how many times you will start out 0–1? A lot. Pitchers are not dummies. If you show a tendency, believe me they will try to exploit it.

On the other hand, if you are known for crushing the first pitch fastball, two things could happen. One, they won't give you a very good pitch to hit very often, which means you will probably be ahead in the count 1–0 (depending on the umpire, or the quality of the pitch). Or two, you will see plenty of breaking and off-speed pitches on the first pitch. Which, again, the smart hitter can adjust to.

NOTE

◆ ◆ ◆ ◆ ◆ ◆ ◆ ◆

Rickey Henderson is the most prolific first-pitch hitter that ever lived. He has more first-pitch, first at-bat home runs than any player in the history of the game. Rickey is not considered a power hitter. How then is he able to hold this distinction? Because he is a smart hitter. He looks for that grooved fastball on the first pitch. When he gets it, he pounces on it!

Baseball is
90% Mental

UMPIRES

One more reason to pay attention when you are not at the plate is the umpires. When you are in the dugout, the on-deck circle, and even out in the field, pay attention to what the umpire calls a strike. Every umpire has his own view of the "strike zone." Some call the strikes high, some low, some outside. My experience has been that the low ball is "called" more often than any pitch.

Pay attention. If you see that all game long the umpire has been calling batters out on a pitch very low in the strike zone, don't think he won't call *you* out on the same pitch!

If you are at bat late in a game and have a two-strike count, you should "look" for something low in the zone. I guarantee you that the catcher has been paying attention to "called" strikes the whole game long. He knows a low pitch will probably be called for a strike. Even if there is a different pitcher in the game, the catcher will probably ask for a pitch very low in the zone. If you can't hit this pitch, foul it off. Battle. Like I've said before, sooner or later that pitcher will make a mistake. Then you hit him.

Being a smart hitter is a big part of being successful at the plate. Pay attention, it pays off.

HIT TO YOUR STRENGTHS

Do you hit the high ball better than the low ball? The inside pitch better

than the outside pitch? Are you better at hitting a fastball or something off-speed? Can you hit breaking pitches?

You should *always* go to the plate with a purpose. That purpose should be to hit the pitch you are best at hitting whenever possible. Whatever that pitch is, have the purpose of mind to "look" for it until you have two strikes. You may not get it. Every at-bat is different. But if you are looking for your strength and get it, chances are you will hit it hard somewhere. Sal Maglie, one of the great pitchers in the Babe Ruth era, once said, "You only need two pitches: one they're lookin' for and one to cross them up."

Look for your pitch. You may get the perfect pitch but miss it completely. Or you may pop it straight up (Fig. 7-1). That is part of baseball. Hitting is a difficult thing. You will fail much more often than you succeed. It's the nature of the game. But if you know where your strengths are and get a pitch in that area, you enhance your chance for success.

If you go to the plate with no idea, no purpose, no hitter's mentality, you might as well not play the game. Because hitting is the game! If you can hit, you will play.

Many ball players have played major league baseball through the years. Do you know which ones are remembered? Hitters and pitchers. Don't get me wrong, fielding is a huge part of the game. But the essence of the game is between the

Fig. 7–1

hitter and the pitcher. Have a purpose when you stride to the plate. Be remembered.

SITUATIONAL HITTING

Most coaches are going to tell you what they want you to do in a particular at-bat when a game is on the line. Whether the sign be "hit away," "bunt," "hit and run," or whatever, your job will be to understand the situation and execute the play accordingly. The various chapters in this book discuss the techniques for bunting, pulling the ball, and hitting the other way.

Baseball is
90% Mental

77

When situational hitting, you must adopt whichever technique best helps the team to succeed—not you as an individual. The team comes first.

THE HIT AND RUN

If you are given the "hit and run" sign, no matter the count, you should try to hit behind the runner. Try to go the other way if you're a right-handed hitter (Fig. 7-2) or pull the ball if you are a lefty. In addition,

Fig. 7–2

in order to protect the runner, you must do your best to get your bat on the ball. Track that ball intensely and get it in play. Advancing the runner is your goal. If you make an out and still advance the runner, you have succeeded. Unless, of course, that out is the third one.

Remember this: Only the best hitters get asked to execute the "hit and run." If the coach believes in you, believe in yourself. If you get the "hit and run" sign, take a second to pump yourself up with a positive thought. Step out of the batter's box, take a deep breath, and say something positive to yourself. Major league players do this all the time. That positive statement, or thought, may help you succeed.

SACRIFICE BUNT/SQUEEZE PLAY

The techniques for bunting are found in the next chapter of this book. In regard to situational hitting, the hitter must realize that the outcome of the game may rest on his ability to successfully lay down a bunt. Late in a game you may be asked to move a runner into scoring position by bunting. You absolutely must be able to execute this when called on. Failure in these situations generally disintegrates an inning and sometimes kills the momentum of a team.

I guarantee you that if you get the job done when asked to bunt, every player on the team will slap you on the back and greet you with "high-fives." It is a critical aspect of the game. Study the chapter on bunting and learn to do it well.

THE SACRIFICE FLY

This is one situation you won't get a sign for. You must know the game well enough to recognize the situation when it arises. If you are batting in the third, fourth, fifth, or sixth spot in your team's lineup, you have shown the tendency to hit for power. Otherwise, you probably would not bat in that position. Therefore, if you ever come to the plate with less than two outs and a runner standing at third base, you must drive this run in.

The sacrifice fly is one way to do so. Go back to the section on pitch counts (see pages 73–75) and your strengths (see pages 76–77). What do you hit best? If you drive the "middle-in" pitch into the gap 90% of the time, look for it. Get the runner in. If you know which pitches you tend to hit in the air, and you have less than two strikes on you, you should be looking to crush one of these pitches. You don't really care if they catch it. If you hit it hard enough, the runner will score. That's your job. Plain and simple. Score the runner.

If you happen to hit the ball in the gap for extra bases, great! But in these situations you absolutely must have a purpose. You must look for a pitch (up until two strikes) that you can "drive." If you have no purpose in these situations, you will likely fail to score the runner. You will just go up there and flail away. You may succeed and you may not. But if you go up there with a purpose, a goal, your chance for success is more likely.

Know the game. Take it upon yourself to recognize what your team needs. Get the job done. Be remembered.

HITTING BREAKING PITCHES

You are probably wondering why I chose to include this topic in this chapter. After all, it should be instructional, right? Well, yes and no. It has been my experience that learning to hit a curve, slider, or off-speed pitch is more of a mental process than a physical one. Once you have established a fundamentally sound swing and proven your ability to hit fastballs, there is no reason that you cannot hit a curve ball as well—except if you think you can't! If you think you can't, then you're done—Finis! Kaput! History! You must believe in yourself as a hitter. Believe and you can achieve!

Understanding the Pitch

There are certain mental aspects to hitting that you must understand in order to hit breaking and off-speed pitches. Read again the section on tendencies and pitch counts (see pages 73–75). You have to know these tendencies, and the tendencies of the pitcher. This is vital information for the hitter.

For younger players, unless you are playing on a club team, you probably won't see much more than a fastball and change-up until you are nearly 13 years old. However, in AAU, AABC, CABA, or other-type club teams, you could start seeing change-ups and curveballs as early as age 10.

At this age, the pitchers are still learning to control these pitches. For the most part, you will not see any-

Baseball is 90% Mental

thing off-speed unless the pitcher is ahead in the count—most likely only when he has you in the hole (0–2 or 1–2). For a young hitter, this is a good time to be aware of the curve or the off-speed pitch. This is the first phase of learning to hit these pitches.

If you have been paying attention to the game and the pitcher, and not clowning around in the dugout between at-bats, you should know if the pitcher has been throwing a change-up or a curve when he has two strikes on the batter. If he has, you should be aware of it. If you are, you will probably hit it. You should still "look" for the fastball and "adjust" to the curve. You simply cannot catch up to a good fastball if you are "looking" for a curve. But you should be aware of the tendency of certain pitchers to throw curve or off-speed balls in those situations. Your awareness could help you adjust and prevent you from looking foolish.

For older players, especially from high school on up, you may get the curve in more diverse situations. But, if you pay attention, you will see that the tendencies described earlier still hold true.

Recognizing the Pitch

The second phase of hitting a curveball is to recognize it. Many hitters claim to be able to see a "button" on the side of breaking pitches. You may be able to. I always judge the speed of the ball as it approaches the plate and its flight path, or trajectory. If you recognize the speed, you keep your timing intact. And that, my friend, is vital.

Once you have recognized the change of speed, your goal is to stay back, stay "loaded." For as long as possible, stay back. Let the ball travel to you. Do not reach for it. Let it travel and track it intently. Accelerate your hands to the ball. Do not slow your hands down because the ball is going slower. That is an easy way to get yourself out. Use a quick bat through the zone—really accelerate the swing and punish the curveball for being hittable.

Thirdly, and here is the key, if, when you recognize it as a "spinner"—the ball being at least belt high—take a whack at it. Let it travel to you and hit it hard. The ball must be "up in the zone" when you detect it as a curve, especially when you are learning to hit one. If it is lower than your belt, let it go by, unless you have two strikes. The spin of the ball will accentuate its downward path and it will more than likely drop out of the strike zone. If it's "up," hit it. If it's "down," let it pass.

Taking the Swing

When you do swing at a curve, remember that it is going to change direction. To better track the flight of the ball, you must minimize head movement. If you jar yourself with a big heavy step (lunging at the ball), you will lose track for a fraction of a second. That's all it takes to miss the pitch. Stay back for as long as possible, take a light step, and keep your front shoulder "in." Swing to the spot you calculate the ball will *be,* not to the spot where the ball *is.*

There is an old saying in baseball: "Hit high breaking balls and low fast ones." As a general rule of thumb, "slow" and "low" do not mix. The reason is gravity. The earth pulls a slow moving object toward the ground. If it is already "low," gravity will pull it even lower before it reaches the hitting zone. A fast moving ball is less affected by gravity.

If you are facing a pitcher that throws plenty of off-speed and breaking stuff, think "no-slow-low." Remind yourself not to swing at those pitches until you have two strikes. Even with two strikes, you should track the slow, low pitch as long as possible. Swing only at the last instant if you think it could be a strike. Maybe you will foul it off and force him to throw you a better pitch. Low breaking pitches are very difficult to hit consistently. Even the greatest of hitters seldom hit these pitches. Get a better pitch to hit.

The Formula for Curveballs

1. **Be aware**

    a. Know the pitcher

    b. Know the pitch count

    c. Know tendencies

2. **Recognize**

    a. The speed is the key

    b. Look for spin (button)

3. **Location**

    a. At least belt high

4. **Track flight**

    a. Steady head

    b. Stay back

    c. Step softly

    d. Accelerate the swing

Baseball is
90% Mental

chapter 8
THE ART OF
BUNTING

There are a number of situations that could arise in a game that might require a batter to bunt the ball to help his team win. Being able to bunt effectively makes a hitter invaluable to his team. Hitters must understand that a great bunt can be as important as a home run.

THE SACRIFICE BUNT

There are several types of bunts, the most basic of which is the sacrifice bunt. On the sacrifice bunt, the hitter's responsibility is to move a runner from first to second, or from second to third. The name of the play, "sacrifice," tells you that as a hitter

you are giving yourself up for the team. You are essentially allowing the defense to get you out while at the same time moving a teammate into scoring position.

This is the easiest of bunts to execute. To get in position for this bunt, you can choose from two styles: the "pivot" or the "square."

To "pivot," the hitter merely "squashes the bug" with his back foot while simultaneously rotating his front foot toward the pitcher (Fig. 8-1). The hitter's belt buckle, chest, and feet are facing the pitcher. The batter keeps his knees bent in a balanced, athletic position.

Fig. 8–1

To "square" around, the batter must position himself properly in the batter's box. The batter must stand slightly farther away from the plate than normal. He pivots on his front foot and brings his rear foot forward

Fig. 8–2a

Fig. 8–2b

Fig. 8–2c

until he is "square" to the pitcher (Figs. 8-2a,b,c). By squaring in this manner, the batter is closer to the plate and to the front, which allows him a better chance to get the bunt down fair. You want to bunt the ball in front of the plate. If the ball meets the bat over the plate, there is a good chance that it could go foul. Try to meet the ball in front.

If the batter squares around by pulling the front foot back, he finds himself much farther from the front of the plate and unable to reach the outside pitch. You want to bunt the ball before it reaches the plate. By squaring with the rear foot coming forward, you are in a more advantageous position to do so. Be certain you leave your-

The Art of
Bunting

self enough room so as not to step on the plate.

At the same time the hitter is making his pivot or square, he releases the bat with his top hand. The hitter makes a "thumbs-up" sign (Fig. 8-3) and slides the top hand up the barrel of the bat. The bat rests on the index finger (Fig. 8-4) and the thumb is placed behind the bat for support. The player should hold the bat lightly and extend the bat out in front of him, leaving the arms slightly flexed (Fig. 8-5).

For most bunts, the hitter must concentrate on not allowing the barrel of the bat to drop lower than the handle (Fig. 8-6). The bat should initially be positioned at the top of the strike zone. The hitter does not adjust to the height of the pitch by merely moving his arms or the bat. He must adjust to the height of the pitch by using his legs. For a low ball, he squats more, bringing the bat down into the path of the ball (Fig. 8-7). In no instance should you attempt to bunt a ball that is higher than your hands. Place the bat at the top of the strike zone and adjust "down," not "up." If you try to bunt a ball that is higher than your hands you will likely pop it up for an easy out.

The batter should try to make contact with the ball between the end of the bat and his top hand (Fig. 8-8), preferably within the last 4 inches of the bat. The farther toward the end of the bat the ball strikes, the softer it comes off the bat.

Fig. 8–3

Fig. 8–4

Fig. 8–5

Fig. 8–6

Fig. 8–7

Fig. 8–8

The Art of
Bunting

Fig. 8–9

Fig. 8–10

The lower hand is used to guide the direction of the bunt. For a bunt down the third base line (for righties), the lower hand is pulled back slightly, creating an angle off the face of the bat that sends the ball toward third base (Fig. 8-9). To go the opposite way, the same hitter would push the handle slightly toward the pitcher (Fig. 8-10). This creates the proper angle to send the ball down first base.

For the "sacrifice bunt" there is no reason to delay getting in the proper position. You are not trying to disguise your intent to lay down the bunt. You really don't care if everybody in the ballpark knows. Get in position to bunt as soon as the pitcher begins his motion to the plate. The sooner you are in position, the better your ability to adjust to the pitch.

On the "bunt and run" or the "squeeze bunt," you should disguise your intent to bunt for as long as possible. Preferably, the ball should be released from the pitcher's hand before you "square" to bunt. However, in *all* cases, the *location* of the bunt is more important than the surprise.

THE SQUEEZE BUNT

The squeeze is designed to score a runner from third base with less than two outs. The runner is totally dependent on the batter to successfully make contact with the pitch. He begins charging home from third the moment the pitcher commits to delivering the ball, just as if he were trying to steal home. If the

Fig. 8–11

BUNTING FOR A HIT

batter is unable to bunt the ball, there is a good chance the runner will be out at home.

If either the batter or the runner reveals the play too soon, a smart pitcher will throw the ball high and inside to a right-handed hitter. The batter's natural reaction is to avoid being hit by the pitch. The catcher merely catches the ball and tags the runner out at home. Try to disguise the squeeze for as long as possible, but be certain you get the bat on the ball. You teammate is relying on you.

The footwork is a little different when a hitter is trying to lay down a bunt for a hit. He must disguise his intentions for as long as possible to keep the fielders from charging in. At the last second, he slides his top hand up the barrel of the bat. For a right-handed hitter, the moment his top hand begins to move, he drops his right foot back, about 6–8 inches, as though he were preparing himself for a sprint (Fig. 8-11). Both actions are done moments before the ball reaches the hitting zone. The batter

The Art of Bunting

89

Fig. 8–12a

Fig. 8–12c

Fig. 8–12b

is actually moving toward first base
as the ball touches the bat. Remember that the direction is supplied by
the actions of the lower hand. You
must read the defense and bunt the
ball accordingly.

If the hitter sees the pitcher charging particularly hard, he could choose
to "push" the ball past him. To do
this, the hitter punches his hands at
impact. This little punching action
will provide enough momentum for
the ball to travel past the pitcher's
mound. If you can do that, you have
a good chance of reaching base safely.

The left-handed batter must execute what is called a "crossover"
step (Figs. 8-12a,b,c) when bunting
for a hit. As the pitch reaches the

hitting zone, the hitter pivots on the front foot and brings the left foot over toward the pitcher. He is actually getting a running start for first base. This is referred to as a "drag" bunt, because the hitter literally drags the bat behind him, leaving it in the hitting zone for as long as possible as he sprints toward first base. Good left-handed bunters have a huge advantage because of this technique, plus the fact that they start out closer to first base. Even if the defense is expecting the bunt it is hard to defend against a good bunter from the left side of the plate.

THE BUTCHER BOY

There is one other play worth mentioning here. Often times in a close game the mental aspect of the game can be very interesting. Cat and mouse games get played between the opposing managers. Is he going to steal, hit and run, bunt, hit away?

What is he up to over there?

The same deception can be played at the plate if the hitter is capable of handling the bat. The butcher boy play is one where the situation calls for the hitter to bunt. The batter intentionally squares around early to deceive the fielders. Naturally, they charge in to protect against the bunt. At the last instant, the batter slides the top hand back down to the handle and takes a swing at the ball. He does not change the position of his feet. There is no need to hit the ball for power. With the defense on the move, it doesn't take much to get the ball past them.

The butcher boy play is very effective even if the hitter happens to miss. The next time the hitter squares to bunt, the fielders will be a little more careful about how quickly they charge in for the bunt. The cat and mouse portion of the game is in full swing. Will he bunt? Will he hit? Only the butcher boy knows.

The Art of
Bunting

chapter 9
HANDLING
FAILURE

The proper mental attitude for a hitter is to first understand that you will fail more times than you succeed. Notice I didn't say *accept* failure; I said *understand* that you will fail. There is a big difference between the two.

To illustrate the difficulty of hitting a pitched ball, the greatest hitters that ever played the game "failed" nearly seven of every ten times they stepped to the plate! The last player to hit for an average of .400 or better was Ted Williams, in 1941! Nearly 60 years have passed. Since then every player has failed a minimum of 60% of the time. Every single player for nearly 60 years has failed more often than he has succeeded!

That said, what is failure? In the scene I described in the previous chapter about the hitter who made an out moving his teammate into scoring position, did he fail? According to his batting average, he did. But every member of his team congratulated him. This player did not fail. Just because you do not reach base safely does not mean you fail.

When you look at a Strike Three with two outs and the bases loaded, with the outcome of the game on the line, you have failed. You know what? It's going to happen. Nobody is perfect. If you swing at that same pitch and miss, have you failed? Yes.

Should you stomp to the dugout, throw your bat and helmet, and kick everything in sight? Never.

Don't think you have to show everybody in the whole world that you are upset at your failure to produce. Trust me, everyone in the ballpark knows how you feel. It isn't necessary to show them. You tried, you failed. All done, can't change it. Can't go back and do it again. It's over, forget it, and move on. Did I say *accept* it? No. *Understand* that failure is part of the game.

What I tell young players is this: If you tried your best and failed, that's the way it goes. Grab the barrel of your bat, run to the dugout, and say these words: "I'll get 'em next time!" Say them out loud.

This is what is known as positive affirmation. You are telling yourself that you will do better next time. Be positive. Nothing negative should ever be spoken by a ball player on a ball field. Positive thoughts and positive statements get positive results. If you learn at an early age to grab the barrel of the bat and run to the dugout with a positive outlook, you will carry that approach with you wherever you go. In competition or in life—get 'em next time.

Here's another scenario for you: Let's say it is late in the game, the score is tied, the winning run is on third, and you are up to bat. You really smash the ball. The ball is sizzling towards center field. The shortstop comes out of nowhere and makes a diving catch. You're out! Did you fail? No. Does your batting average say you failed? Yes.

Success and failure are not dictated by your batting average. Don't get caught up in that. Your goal as a hitter is to go to the plate with a purpose, get a good pitch to hit, and hit it hard somewhere. Sometimes it will find a hole and sometimes it will find a glove. You have not failed if you hit the ball. Don't hang your head or cry the blues. If the defense makes a good play, tip your hat. Your job is to hit the ball, his is to field it. "Get 'em next time!" If you maintain that even keel, you will be a better ball player because of it.

There is a tremendous amount of emotion in the game of baseball—moreso late in a game if the score is close. But throwing and kicking and spewing negative statements won't change anything that has happened. Understand that the greatest players in the game fail more times than they succeed. Focus your energy on what is ahead, not on what has already happened. What can you do to be successful the next time you come to bat? Think positive. Be positive. You'll be a better ball player and a much better person.

INDEX

ABOUT THE AUTHOR

Buz Brundage started coaching baseball in 1981. He initially became involved as a community service endeavor by helping out one of the local little leagues and eventually became more involved when he saw the positive impact he had on so many young men's lives. He has coached AAU, AABC, and local club teams. As an assistant coach, he helped lead a team to a berth in the AABC World Series.

Buz is married with three children: Derek, 17, Bryon, 12—each having already competed in National Baseball Championship events—and Keli, 9, who swings a pretty good bat as well.

Buz is a former United States Marine and a 20-year veteran of the Las Vegas Metropolitan Police Department. He continues to coach baseball year round.